Never Again . . .

A Love Story

by R. M. Flansburg

Mavis Stevens, Illustrator

Never Again . . . A Love Story

Copyright © 2015

R. M. Flansburg

All Rights Reserved

Library of Congress Control Number
2015911816

ISBN # 978-0-692-46612-4

Contact the author or order additional copies at:
GraftonLoveStory@gmail.com

Printed in the USA by
Morris Publishing®
3212 E Hwy 30
Kearney, NE 68847
800-650-7888   www.morrispublishing.com

To

LaVern and Suzie White

Acknowledgments

Thanks be to God for his guiding hand in the writing of this book.

Throughout my many years of studying the Holocaust and the ramifications of this terrible period in the history of humankind, God, in his infinite wisdom, has been my rock and fortress, a very present help in trouble and has proceeded to open doors for me, that I didn't even know existed.

Praise God from whom all blessings flow!

Without Linda Koschmeder, who served as formatter, compiler, general supporter and cheerleader, this book would not have been possible. When my writing came to a standstill due to losing my beloved husband to cancer, she helped me pick up the pieces of my life. Her commitment to my dream, her belief that I had a message that needed to be heard, brought me back to the land of the living. She was the voice of God's love, reminding me of God's abundant grace and his abiding love for me in all times and places.

Mavis Stevens, who created all the illustrations for *Never Again*, is also one of God's great gifts. Her drawings capture both the violence of life lived under Nazi domination and the contrasting tenderness of young love blossoming amidst the rubble left in the wake of the war. Her support and never failing appreciation for my vision saw me through many dark days. God has blessed her with a wonderful talent that she joyfully shares, and thus we have been blessed.

I will be forever grateful to Dr. Eugene Kreider, the professor that taught the Holocaust class that changed my life and set me on the path that eventually led to the writing of this book.

Through him, and the materials to which the class was exposed, I found myself drawn into the horror and the pathos of the events of those terrible years. I felt as though the Holocaust became my experience, as I wrestled with the question, "Why was I born in safety? Why were other children marked for death, even before they were brought into this world?"

Daily I thank God for his gift of my family and friends, too numerous to mention by name, whose support and encouragement has been so overwhelming, especially after the death of my husband.

Finally, thank you to LaVern and Suzie White who welcomed me into their home and hearts, sharing with me some things they had never before shared with anyone else. I am honored and humbled by their faith and trust in me. I have tried to handle their disclosures with dignity and respect. Theirs is a story to treasure, unique unto its time and place. How blessed am I to have been given the privilege of committing it to pen, paper, and computer.

The Lord works in mysterious ways, his wonders to perform.

Table of Contents

Preface 8

Introduction 12

  Poem - *February, 1942* 15

Chapter 1 – Blitzkrieg 17

  A HISTORY - On Being Chosen 23

    Reflections 25

      Poem - *The Chosen* 26

Chapter 2 – Occupation 29

  A HISTORY - The Devil's Advocate 32

    Reflections 34

      Poem - *The Jew* 35

Chapter 3 – Preparing for the Unknown 37

  Poem - *The Wind - Always the Wind* 42

  A HISTORY - The Road to Power and Domination 46

    Reflections 47

Chapter 4 – The Guilt and Shame of Silence 49

  A HISTORY - The Deceitful Path to Dehumanization 51

    Reflections 52

      Poem - *On Roosters* 53

        Reflections - Why the Silence 54

Chapter 5 – The Reality of War 57

  A HISTORY - Sinking Into The Abyss 62

Chapter 6 – Resistance, Frustration, and Weariness 65

  A HISTORY - The Beginning of the End for Adolf Hitler ..67

Chapter 7 – Buchenwald 69

   Reflections on Buchenwald 72

      Poem - *Auschwitz* 73

         A HISTORY - The Final Solution 76

            Reflections 77

               Poem - *Trains* 79

Chapter 8 – Liberation 81

   A HISTORY - The Twilight of the Gods 84

      Reflections 85

Chapter 9 – The Wonder of Spring 87

   A HISTORY - The Holocaust 91

Chapter 10 – When the Love Bug Bites, It Really Bites Hard. .93

   Reflections on the Holocaust 97

Chapter 11 – Getting to Know You 99

Chapter 12 – Love Makes the World Go Round 105

   Questions That Arose From the Ashes 111

Chapter 13 – The Impossible Dream? 113

   Questions That Arose From the Ashes 118

Chapter 14 – Separation 121

   Questions That Arose From the Ashes 126

Chapter 15 – As Time Goes By 129

Chapter 16 – The New World 133

   Questions That Arose From the Ashes 138

Epilog 140

Conclusion 144

Preface

I first became interested in the Holocaust after spending a day at Dachau Concentration Camp, located near Munich, Germany. It was a very sobering experience. During the year and a half that I lived in that country, World War II, its history and the questions that arose concerning the presence of God in our suffering became a consuming interest of mine.

Twenty years later, having decided to pursue a career in Christian ministry, I enrolled as a student at Luther Seminary, in St. Paul, Minnesota. I discovered that the school offered a course on the Holocaust, and I immediately registered for it.

Dr. Eugene Kreider was the professor. He was a very quiet man, who spoke eloquently about the terrible atrocities that occurred during that period in the history of humankind. We studied the development of Anti-Semitism, and were introduced to the literature that the Holocaust generated. Many survivors visited our class and told us of their personal experiences and we were given the opportunity to interact with them as they shared their stories. We also attended worship at a local synagogue and participated in one of their festival celebrations.

I felt myself being drawn into the pathos, horror and tragedy of the Holocaust in such away, that it became my experience, as much as is possible that is, for a Scandinavian "Aryan."

Being a Christian, my personal faith is very different from that of the children of Israel, or so I thought. However, Dr. Kreider enabled me to understand more deeply that beneath the color of our skin and behind the shape of our eyes, we are the same. In our humanity we are all interconnected. As a human being I love, I hate, I think, I laugh, I experience sorrow and joy, I feel pain, I bleed, I cry. Therefore, in my humanity, the Holocaust becomes my experience.

I was surprised at how deeply my research affected me. The more I studied the happenings of those terrible years, the more emotional I became. I knew I must share what was happening in the depths of my being, thus I turned to poetry. It is a literary form that enables one to speak the language of the soul.

The poems in this book are my attempt to convey the passion that has become mine as a result of my journey through the Holocaust.

A very meaningful component in our study of the Holocaust was an introduction to the Lament Psalms, which are seldom read and studied as they demonstrate a very different view of the life of faith. With a boldness that is only found elsewhere in Bible in the book of Job, they cry out to the LORD, "Where are you God in my suffering?"

These Psalms speak to the agonized soul, giving the believer permission to be mad at God and to verbalize that anger. They enable us to recognize that those emotions are valid and are part of the walk of faith. The Lament Psalms show us what it is to be human and they embrace our "humanness."

With the exception of two or three of the Laments, they follow a distinct pattern. The Psalm begins with a cry against the LORD.

"My God, My God, why have you forsaken me?" (Psalm 22:1, Jesus' words on the cross.)

In the middle section of a Lament Psalm the writer continues to expound on his sorrow and feelings of abandonment. This conversation proves to be very therapeutic. He begins to remember God's promises of God's faithfulness and in so doing he realizes that he has not been abandoned. God has been there, though silent, throughout his whole time of pain and sorrow.

The last section of the Lament is one of joy and thanksgiving for rediscovering God's abundant grace and faithful presence.

"You who fear the LORD, praise him! . . . he did not hide his face from me, but heard when I cried to him." Psalm 22:23-24

Chapters 1-8 tell of the horror of of living under Nazi domination and being witness to the atrocities committed during that time, thus I introduce each chapter with words of suffering as voiced by the Psalmist.

Chapters 9-16 narrate the long road back, after the end of the war to so-called normalcy, with the recognition that nothing will ever be the same again. Consequently each chapter is prefaced by words of thanksgiving, uttered in joy by the Psalmist.

As one comes face to face with the horrors of the Holocaust, and we in turn, experience the sorrows and difficulties that are encountered in everyday living, the Lament Psalms can become surprisingly comforting. They are a source of strength, hope and reality. They "tell like it is!" They show us that God is real and that knowledge consequently, enables us to be real and honest in our relationship with our Lord.

After finishing the class I continued my work on the Holo-caust by completing a directed independent study on the subject under Dr. Kreider's supervision. The research materials gathered during that study provided the basis for the theological questions that I raise for discussion and contemplation in this book.

Upon my graduation from the seminary and being ordained in the Evangelical Lutheran Church in America, I accepted a call to serve two country churches in northern Iowa. The call also in-cluded my being the visitation pastor at a church in the nearby farming community of Grafton. It was in that capacity that I came to know LaVern and Suzie White.

LaVern and Suzie White are long time residents of the small farming community of Grafton. They are a quiet and unassuming couple who appear to have lived very ordinary lives. Nothing could be farther from the truth.

LaVern is a World War II veteran, who served in the European theater. As a soldier in General Patton's Third Army he survived the "Battle of the Bulge," and many ensuing engagements. Suzie is a native of Belgium, and came to the United State as a "war bride." Their love affair is the stuff out of which movies are made. On becoming acquainted with LaVern and Suzie and hearing their story, I knew I must, with their permission, share their incredible journey.

I tell the story of their love, the obstacles they had to overcome to see it to fruition and their dreams for the future, in parallel with the six million who also loved and dreamed and *did not survive.*

Unfortunately before I could finish writing their story, LaVern passed from this life. However, I had extensive notes from the many conversations we had together, and thus I was able to complete the saga of their love and those momentous times in which they lived.

During my many visits with LaVern, he often became very emotional as he shared his grief and sorrow over the events he had witnessed. Even though he is no longer with us, I decided to leave his words of deep sadness in the present tense just as I first heard them. The use of the present tense creates an authenticity that lends credence to his narrative and heightens the drama surrounding LaVern and Suzie.

As I worked to share their incredible journey, I was continually aware of the six million who also dreamed and made plans for the future; the six million who were exterminated before they could live out their dreams.

It is my hope that this writing will prompt, yet, another generation to say *"Never Again . . . Never Again!"*

Introduction

It was the war that stripped away all the trappings of innocence and revealed the evil that lurks barely beneath the surface of all humankind. It made men out of boys, mechanics out of women and monsters out of the mediocre.

It was the war that desensitized the human race to pain and agony inflicted upon others who were considered "different." As the smoke from the belching furnaces of Nazi Germany's death camps rose into the air, filling the atmosphere with the putrid smell of burning flesh, few in the surrounding countryside took notice. They became used to the stench, and the sounds, and pretended all was normal.

It was the war that changed the world's view; that the end justifies the means; for those who witnessed the atrocity of dehumanization and genocide, and did not turn their backs, cried out, **"Never again! Never again!"**

It was the war that engulfed all of the northern hemisphere, so broad in scope that it became known as World War II, or as some have called it: the last "just" war.

Seven years the battles raged in places before unknown to us, with names that were strange and different: Midway, Iwo Jima, Omaha Beach, Anzio, Guadalcanal, Tobruk, The Battle of the Bulge. Then there were other places, never to be forgotten, as the liberating troops were marched to the gates of hell, ushered into the depths of human depravity and brought face to face with the ugliness of the demon that dwells in each of us.

"Who is responsible?"

"Wherein lies responsibility?"

"Why did God allow this to happen?"

"Where is God?"

"Why me?"

"Why not me?"

These were the questions that arose from the ashes of the Nazi death camps of Auschwitz, Treblinka, Bergen-Belsen, and Buchenwald: questions that continue to haunt.

February, 1942

A child was born,
A beautiful little girl,
Loved by adoring parents,
Warm . . . safe . . . nurtured . . . protected.

A child was born,
A beautiful little girl,
One who would have been loved by her adoring parents,
Cold . . . in danger . . . alone . . . at risk.

Years of life ahead for the little girl,
Safe . . . warm . . . protected,
Suckled by her mother's breast.

Minutes of life ahead for the little girl,
In danger . . . alone . . . at risk,
Ripped from her mother's arms.

Soft cuddly, blankets,
Enfolding arms.

A bed of human flesh,
The consuming fire of a belching furnace.

Why me?
Why her?

R. M. Flansburg, born February 1, 1942
An unknown child, born February 1, 1942

Vindicate me, O God, and defend my cause against an ungodly people; from those who are deceitful and unjust deliver me!

For you are the God in whom I take refuge; why have you cast me off? Why must I walk about mournfully because of the oppression of the enemy?

Psalm 43:1-2

Chapter 1 – Blitzkrieg

"Bang . . . Bang . . . Bang . . . ! Bombs were exploding everywhere. There was no place to hide, no place to run. I was terrified . . . the horror of that day continues to haunt my dreams and it has been seventy years!" says Belgium *World War II* bride, Suzie White, as she shuttered in remembrance.

"They killed her . . . they killed my best friend," she continues. "I will never forget seeing it happen right in front of me. Even now, whenever I think of that terrible day I am filled with hate and fear. What had we done to deserve this? What were we to the Germans that they had to invade our country and take it from us and kill and maim? No warning, none whatsoever, they just came and bombed and bombed and bombed."

Bang . . . Bang . . . Bang . . . ! Fourteen year old Zanne, and the few remaining diners in her mother's cafe all looked at each other, startled, and wondering what had broken the quiet reverie that comes after a meal that fills and satisfies. What was that noise? From where did it come?

[Zanne is pronounced zah nah - with the ah like a in father. This is the name her family always called her. Her given name is Suzanne. Suzie became her American name when LaVern's family met her at the train station in Iowa.]

Bang . . . Bang . . . Bang . . . ! Again that explosive sound, followed by the drone of airplane engines. Out into the street they ran, their eyes turned to the sky. What they saw struck terror in their hearts. Flying directly over them were German war planes! Zanne stood transfixed, as bombs fell all about her. In horror, she helplessly watched as her best friend was hit by flying shrapnel, killing her instantly. It was a day she would never forget, a day burned into her memory, May 10, 1940.

Fear and loathing consumed her as she viewed the devastation surrounding her, in the wake of the German attack. The townspeople had heard about "BLITZKRIEG" [massive bombing raids with no previous warning, followed by German infantry killing and maiming everything in their path], now it was their experience, their town, their friends, their loved ones, caught in the horror of BLITZKRIEG. As the residents of the little factory town of Rieme-Ertvelde, Belgium beheld the destruction and the smoke rising from the craters left by the bombs, they began to realize their world would never be the same. The terror Zanne experienced and hatred born in her during those fateful moments remain with her, an ever fresh memory that creeps into her daily living and causes her to ask, "How could God allow this to happen?"

Memories of her life before that fateful day are fuzzy and remote. It is as if she had lived a pre-birth, womb-like existence until the BLITZKRIEG, when she was birthed into a world of brutality, the realization of which shook her to the very depths of her fourteen-year-old being.

One of nine children, born to devout Catholic parents, Zanne spent her early years at a convent school, where two of the nuns were her aunts. With those two aunts watching her every move. "I had to be on my best behavior," she has been heard to say, many times, with an accompanying little chuckle. The convent was a distance from her town, thus she stayed at the school Monday through Friday, returning home for weekends. It was a safe and secure existence. All she really had to worry about were those two ever seemingly present aunts!

Her family's life was centered around the cafe which they owned and operated. It was appropriately named "The Anchor," as it was located in the heart of the factory district facing one of the many canals that traversed the town. It was well frequented, by the workers in the area, especially at noon.

Being only fourteen, Zanne was considered too young to work in the dining room, but was involved in the operation of the eatery in various other ways.

Not only was the cafe their livelihood, it was also their home. The kitchen was the center of family life. The bedrooms were located right above it on the second floor of the building. The factories were their neighbors, and they actually shared a wall with the business next door.

When war broke out in Europe Zanne's mother insisted that she return home from school every evening, which presented transportation problems, but was doable. On May 20, 1940, however, everything changed. Zanne's mother decided that she must leave the convent school and remain at home as she was concerned for her safety in the light of the frequent bombing raids.

Another change concerned their food sources which were suddenly, greatly diminished as the Germans commandeered the best of the meat and vegetables for their soldiers, leaving the Belgians with little or nothing at all. This made life very difficult for her family as their cafe was increasingly becoming popular with the German troops. Though liquor was readily available, they found themselves resorting to the black market for food supplies and also relying on farmers who were able to hide some of their harvest from the invaders, saving what they could for their loyal and long time customers. It was a tricky and dangerous existence for all who were involved. For the first time in her young life Zanne knew real fear and that fear became her constant companion.

Due to the location of the cafe, so close to the factories, the bombings in their area continued until the Germans occupied all of Belgium: thus gaining control of the huge oil reserves that were stored there.

Upon securing the reserves, the German bombings came to a halt. The peace and quiet that accompanied the cessation of the attacks was short-lived, however. The British and the Americans soon began bombing raids of their own, targeting the nearby factories in hopes of slowing down the German war effort. The British bombed by night and the Americans by day, thus blurring the line between friend and foe, rendering the population hopeless, in a stupor of fear and terror.

Having witnessed the bomb's destructive might, Zanne's family decided to build a small bomb shelter in their backyard. "It wasn't much, just a hole in the ground, with stuff on top of it," she says with a slight smile. Their neighbors had a much better shelter, which they tried to reach when the raids would begin, but often they only had time to get to their little hole. In they would jump, hoping it would somehow protect them. Fear encompassed their entire existence, imprisoning them in a hell, not of their own making.

Unlike their neighbors who could shut their doors on the invaders, Zanne's family had to welcome the Germans into their "home," and act as if everything was normal. However, for her family, life was anything but normal. The sight of the military uniforms, the distinctive helmet, the highly polished boots and their abrupt, clipped speech struck terror in the heart of the young girl. Their presence in her "home" was a constant reminder of the tragedy of her best friend's death. That scene played out in her head over and over again, as the trauma invaded her dreams producing terrible nightmares that have never gone away.

As she speaks of this her tears return, the experiences of those years having woven a tapestry of tragedy in the fabric of her life. It is a tapestry of sorrow and grief that abides deep within her inner being and surrounds her with an aura of quiet dignity.

A HISTORY - On Being Chosen

2000 BC

God chooses a wandering nomadic sheep herder and his descendants to be God's chosen people.

Now the Lord said to Abram [later becomes known as Abraham], "Go from your country and your kindred and your father's house to the land that I will show you. I will make of you a great nation, and I will bless you, and make your name great, so that you will be a blessing. I will bless those who bless you, and the one who curses you I will curse; and in you all the families of the earth shall be blessed."

Genesis 12:1-3

33 AD

Jesus Christ is crucified in Jerusalem, at the behest of the Jewish religious leaders, who accuse him of blasphemy (they said he claimed he was God, which according to Jewish law, was a sin punishable by death).

In the centuries that followed, primitive Christian Europe regards the Jew as the "Christ killer," an enemy and a threat to be expelled or be put to death with sword and fire.

1543

The great German theologian and father of the Refor-
mation, Martin Luther, suffers from an acute case of
uremic poisoning which alters his personality, making
him a bitter old man. He strikes out against this mal-
ady by attacking the Jews and sets out his "honest advice" as to how Jews should be treated.

1. Their synagogues should be set on fire.

2. Jewish homes should be broken down or destroyed.

3. Jews should be put under one roof or a stable.

4. Jews should be put to work, to earn their living, "by
   the sweat of their noses."

5. These "poisonous bitter worms" should be stripped
   of their belongs, "which they have exhorted from
   us," and driven out of the country "for all time."

Reflections

"Whatever people God might have chosen would by that act have become different and special and uncommon . . ."

A Holocaust Survivor

"If before the Holocaust the idea that Jews were in some way chosen as merely a myth or legend created by the Jews themselves, then I would say the Nazi program of genocide transformed that fiction into a reality. If we weren't chosen before, we are most certainly chosen now. . . . It is now a down to earth fact for all future time. We Jews are forevermore chosen. The Nazis saw to that."

A Holocaust Survivor

"God chose the Jews to defeat Hitler. If Hitler wasn't entirely and compulsively set upon killing us and expending valuable energy and manpower on this bloody job when he should have used his resources for the war, the Nazis would have won the war. But God hardened his heart as he hardened pharaoh's heart, and we Jews became martyrs again and saved the world from Hitler."

A Holocaust Survivor

The Chosen

I will bless you,
So that you will be a blessing,
And by you all the families of the earth
    shall bless themselves.

Once you were no people,
Now you are God's people.

You did not choose me,
I chose you.

Yes, the Jews are a chosen people,
Chosen, through Abraham,
    for life and blessing by God,
Chosen, at Auschwitz, for death
    and extinction by humankind.

To be chosen,

Blessing or curse?

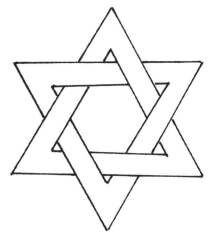

O LORD, do not rebuke me in your anger, or discipline me in your wrath. Be gracious to me, O LORD, for I am languishing; O LORD, heal me, for my bones are shaking in terror. . . . I am weary with my moaning; every night I flood my bed with tears; I drench my couch with my weeping. My eyes waste away because of grief; they grow weak because of all my foes.

Psalm 6:2-3, 6-7

Chapter 2 – Occupation

The clinking of glasses, and the happy chatter that accompanies the eating of a good meal were sounds of normalcy within the walls of the family cafe. It was an island of relative peace, unto itself, while the world outside continued to tear itself apart.

As Zanne grew older, she began working more hours in the dining room, which meant daily contact with the enemy. As she came to know some of the German soldiers, she began to realize that they were people just like her, caught up in a war, not of their own making. She found them to be considerate and very polite. She especially enjoyed one young man who played the piano with great charm and ease, creating lovely background music for their diners.

Getting to know the German soldiers on a more personal basis, however, did not diminish her fear of them, nor lesson her concern about the perilous situation in which her family found itself. Even though she had become friendly with some of the soldiers, she knew she had to watch every word she said. A derogative comment about a German, whispered in the ear by a friend, could be the cause for arrest. To this end the German authorities insisted they post a warning sign on the wall of their cafe that read: ACHTUNG - Watch what you say the enemy will hear you!

Zanne knew this was not an idle threat, as there were shootings every day, often destroying the congenial mood of the diners who were then unable to enjoy the good meal set before them.

While she did not witness the killings, she heard the gunshots. Sometimes it would be civilians that were killed, and other times the resistance would pick off a German soldier here and there. The victims would fall into the canals that crisscrossed their town and about three days later their bloated bodies would float to the surface, creating a terrible stench, a nauseating odor that hung over the dank canals, an ever present reminder that they were an occupied and captive nation.

One day, early in the occupation, she heard the sound of boots pounding on the pavement outside of their cafe, and German voices yelling and screaming. The soldiers were obviously hunting for someone, as they were going door to door, knocking loudly and shouting obscenities. With fear and trembling, Zanne and the diners waited for the soldiers to come storming into the cafe. For some unknown reason, however, just before reaching their building, they moved to the next street over. Zanne could hear the sounds of glass being broken, loud knocking, and more shouting. When no one would divulge the hiding place of the person they were seeking, the Germans randomly selected ten people from the neighborhood, lined them up against a wall and shot them.

While she did not witness the incident with her own eyes the sounds she heard painted a vivid picture in her imagination.

"It was awful," she states, wiping the tears from her eyes. "The fear I experienced that day continues to haunt me. Any loud or unexpected noise will make me jump. It's been more than 70 years and I am still terrorized by that moment of unexplainable and inhumane treatment of innocent people. I became very careful of what I said and to whom I spoke. I found myself continually looking over my shoulder. It was a paralyzing fear that fully consumed me and at times rendered me helpless, with little hope for the future."

Zanne and her family had to be much more careful of what they said and did than many of their neighbors, however, for they harbored a deep, dark secret . . . *Zanne's mother was part Jewish!*

ACHTUNG

Watch what you say

The enemy will hear you!

A HISTORY -
The Devil's Advocate

1889

Adolph Hitler is born.

Due to circumstances in his life he becomes an aggressive and persuasive anti-Semitic, obsessed with the idea that his mission in life is to rid Europe of all Jews.

1921

Hitler becomes a leader in the 'Nazi' Party, the essence of their program is nationalistic: calling for the establishment of a 'Great Germany.' Point Four of their program reads:

"None but members of the Nation may be citizens of the State. None but those of German blood, whatever their creed, may be members of the Nation. No Jew, therefore, may be a member of the Nation."

1923 - 1924

After a failed attempt to seize power in Munich, Hitler is arrested, and tried for high treason, and sentenced to five years in detention. After less than eight months in prison, he is released on parole.

While incarcerated Hitler writes a book, entitled, *Mein Kampf* (My Life).

In the book, he outlines his mission: to expose and destroy the threat posed by a worldwide Jewish effort to destroy the foundations of *Aryan* life.

He believes that Germany's greatness can only be achieved if its people recognize the Jewish danger they are facing.

1925 - 1930

All throughout Germany crowds are mesmerized by Hitler's oratory. **Albert Speer,** who became Hitler's armament minister and chief architect for the Third Reich, tells of this magnetism in his book, *Inside the Third Reich,* which he wrote while serving a twenty year sentence in Spandau prison for war crimes. Albert Speer, at the war crime trials held in Nuremberg, Germany, was the only German official to admit and accept responsibility for the Holocaust.

He was strongly opposed to Hitler and his policies until he attended a rally at Berlin University. Hitler initially spoke with a shyness and a charm that surprised Speer.

"Hitler's initial shyness soon disappeared," Speer states. "At times now his pitch rose. He spoke urgently and with hypnotic persuasiveness. The mood he cast was much deeper than the speech itself, most of which I did not remember for long.

Moreover, I was carried on the wave of enthusiasm one could almost feel physically . . . It swept away any skepticism, any reservations." Speer joined the Nazi party almost immediately.

"By entering Hitler's party I had already, in essence, assumed a responsibility that led directly to the brutalities of forced labor, to the destruction of war, and to the deaths of those millions of so-called undesirable stock – to the crushing of justice and the elevation of every evil."

Reflections

When Hitler spoke about the Jew, he could speak to the Germans in familiar language. When he reviled his victim, he resurrected a medieval conception . . . . The picture of the Jew we encounter in Nazi propaganda and Nazi correspondence had been drawn several hundred years before. Martin Luther had already sketched the main outlines of that portrait and the Nazis in their time had little to add to it.

Raul Hilberg, Jewish Theologian

The Jew

Jesus was a Jew,
Strange to think of him as a Jew.

Jesus was God incarnate, the great "I AM."
Strange to think of him as a Jew.

Jesus drove out demons, healed the sick,
    made the blind to see, and the deaf to hear.

Jesus was crucified as the "King of the Jews,"
Strange to think of him as a Jew.

The Jew was killed at Auschwitz-Birkenau, Cheimo,
Was that Jew, Jesus, King of the Jews?

Strange to think of him as a Jew.

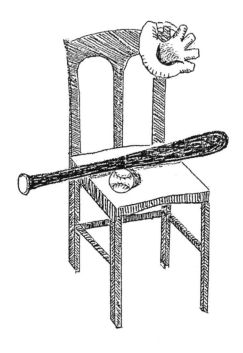

To you, O LORD, I lift up my soul, O my God in you I trust; do not let me be put to shame; do not let my enemies exult over me . . .

Make me to know your ways, O LORD; teach me your paths. Lead me in your truth, and teach me, for you are the God of my salvation; for you I wait all day long.

                                                      Psalm 25:1-2, 4-5

Chapter 3 – Preparing for the Unknown

Before all things there was the wind, always the wind, sweeping across the prairies of Iowa, in constant motion, an entity never seen, rather experienced. It is in its sounds the wind is recognized, as it announces and ushers in the seasons, thus defining the rhythm of life on the prairie and therefore life on the farm.

In the spring, the wind is a gentle breeze, whispering through the prairie grasses, bringing the April showers, nurturing the newly planted crops and emerging buds on the trees. As summer approaches and the leaves and crops mature, the sound of the wind is often a roar as the leaves violently interact with each other and the cornstalks are bowed to the ground by the forces unleashed upon them in a tornado or straight-line wind.

A rustling sound ushers in the fall season as the leaves on the trees become brittle and dry. Cascading to the ground, brilliant in their death, they create a multicolored carpet swept to and fro by the winds of autumn.

The trees left standing, bare and leafless, provide a perfect alleyway for the howling winter winds, sounding forlorn and lonely as the coyotes join their song of snow and cold.

This rhythm of prairie life molds a unique landscape, all its own, creating sturdy, individualists, who farm the land with integrity and are able to cope with almost any circumstance with inventiveness and a self-deprecating sense of humor.

It is a God-fearing culture, steeped in tradition, hard work, and proud patriotism.

It was this culture into which LaVern White was born. He liked to brag that he was born in a bank. The previous owner of the home in which his family lived, was the local banker. When a new and "modern" bank was built in their small farming community, he had the old structure moved out into the country, converting it into a house. Even though they lived in a "bank," theirs was a very meager existence.

Work, work, work, was all LaVern knew his first seventeen years. Being the oldest of six children, responsibility lay heavily upon his shoulders. The "family farm" of the 1930's and 40's required the total commitment of each person in the family in order to "make a go of it."

Farming was and still is, a 24-7 job. There are no weekends off, no quitting time, no stop clock. Cows have to be fed and milked, hogs have to be slopped, chickens fed, eggs gathered and other animals' needs met.

Raising crops adds another dimension to the picture. A farmer is often heard to say, "The good Lord gives us a seed time and a harvest time, and we have to make the most of the time we are granted." Equipment has to be serviced and cleaned and field ready to go when that window of opportunity arises. The soil has to be prepared, seeds planted, and then the fields cultivated. Today pesticides and herbicides are applied to control bugs and weeds, mostly done with huge tractors and applicators. In the 1930's, however, almost everything was done by hand; often with teams of horses. Weeds were controlled by cultivating and hoeing, which was back-breaking work.

Harvest usually began in August, and to bring the crops in was a community effort. All the neighbors would band together to form threshing crews. When the oats were ready, they would go from farm to farm, harvesting the grain. It was a total family effort. Men and boys were in the field and the women cooked and cooked, making meals for the crews. August in Iowa is hot, *hot, hot,* and *very* humid. Early in the morning the cook stove would be fired up and wonderful aromas would soon fill the house as pies and cakes were baked and later served. Yes, it was hot and uncomfortable, but that was life on the farm. Harvest time was labor intensive, but the fellowship that was generated by sharing the workload was very special and bound neighbors together in a way never to be forgotten.

Saturday evening everything came to a halt. Baths were taken (one a week), clean clothes were donned and off to the little nearby town of Grafton went LaVern and his family. It was a time to buy groceries (bought with his mother's saved egg money), to share the happenings of the last week and stories to be told and passed on (farmers never seem to run out of things to talk about).

The evening would end with everyone attending the free movie, which was held on a vacant lot, and shown on a huge white board, made for that purpose. The "movie goers" would sit on planks held up by cement blocks. LaVern loved the Saturday nights spent in town, made all the more special when he would hunt up his grandpa, who when found, would give LaVern a dime and with that he was able to buy an ice cream. What a treat!

He attended the one-room school near him, thus experiencing one of the best elementary educations available in that era. When it came time for him to go to high school, his father insisted that he stay at home, believing an eighth grade education was enough for what he assumed LaVern would be doing in life (farming). His father thought it was time for him to shoulder some heavier responsibilities.

In the middle of October of that year, the superintendent of the Grafton School paid an unexpected visit to the farm and spoke with his father, convincing him that LaVern should finish his schooling. LaVern vividly remembered how difficult it was to start school in October. He was behind in all the subjects and had to work especially hard to catch up with the other students. He wanted to participate in the sports program, but he was far too late for that, plus he had chores to do. However, he was able to play baseball in the spring and discovered that he loved the game.

As soon as he graduated from high school, he enlisted in the army. Japan had attacked Pearl Harbor the previous December and his country was at war. He felt he had no choice. "I had to do what, what I had to do," he stated, not with pride, but with conviction. This is what a young man did. It was his responsibility and he never gave it a second thought. He had been raised in an environment of proud patriotism and now his country needed him and he responded.

The farm, his family, school and Saturday nights in Grafton had been his whole world. They were the parameters of his existence. Overnight everything changed. His enlistment in the army meant leaving behind all he had ever known and saying goodbye to the vast wind-swept prairies of Iowa and the safety net of his family and community.

The army became his family in the following 16 months as he experienced training in various posts throughout the country. A whole new world was opened up to him, a world so interesting and challenging that he hardly had time to be homesick, except at Christmas, which he spent all alone in Tennessee. It was sobering, sad and empty until he began to think about his reasons for "joining up." He had answered a call from his country to help defeat the powers of evil threatening our national freedom. The sense of purpose that had consumed him upon his enlistment again filled his thoughts and he returned to training with a new sense of mission.

The next few months he trained with an anti-aircraft outfit unit at Camp Edwards, Massachusetts, in preparation for action in the European Theater. Upon his arrival in Europe, he was assigned to an Infantry Division which was part of General Patton's Third Army.

In October of 1944, he left the shores of the USA, sailing on the ship the Highland Monarch. They were part of a convoy, making it a fearful voyage as the convoys were constant prey for the German U-boats. For 14 days, he lived on food bought at the ship's PX because the galley was a pit of filth and stench and the food that was served was even worse. The first morning at sea, they were given fish and cooked cabbage for breakfast. Fortunately the Atlantic remained relatively quiet during the entire voyage, which kept troubled stomachs from erupting too much.

They arrived in England safe and unscathed, except for some weight loss and still unsettled stomachs. This "simple" Iowa farm boy had been transformed into a fighting machine, battle ready and scared to death. His whole world had been the little town of Grafton and the family farm. He now stood on the soil of the country that had given birth to America. He would soon experience and witness what no human being should ever experience and witness. Gone forever would be the innocence of the boy who loved to play baseball and was thrilled with a ten cent ice cream.

The Wind - Always the Wind

Before all things there was the wind –
  always the wind
  ever moving
  never seen

Only footprints left in the snowdrifts of winter
Footprints of constant motion
  swirling
  swishing
  swooping
  soaring

The wind – always the wind
the sound of it
  whispering in the prairie grasses
  howling through the barren trees of winter
  roaring like a hungry lion
        TORNADO!   TORNADO!
  rustling the crackling dry leaves
    falling to the ground

  orange
  burgundy
  carpets blown hither and yon in a landscape
  being ever changed by the wind –
Always the wind

And man came
And man saw
And man met the wind and discovered
  friend and foe
  creator and destroyer

And a new landscape appeared
A landscape molded by fear
  fear of the wind –
Always the wind

A landscape of planted fields and shelter belts
Building sights and churchyards guarded by
  mighty trees designed to stop the wind –
Always the wind

And man came
And man met the wind
and man heard
  the whispering
  the howling
  the roaring
  the rustling
The sounds of the wind –
Always the wind

And a new landscape appeared
A landscape molded by the sounds
  of the wind
Sounds of power and might
Sounds of renewal and energy
The wind – always the wind

Mighty turbines appeared on the horizon
Turbines with giant propellers that could
  catch the wind and create

POWER!

Power to light homes and to run factories
A power source that renews itself
The wind –
Always the wind

Before all things there was the wind –
  ever moving
  never seen
  its power proclaimed in its sounds;
  whispering
  howling
  roaring
  and quiet rustling
The power to catch itself –
To renew itself – for the good of all things

The wind – always the wind

A HISTORY -
The Road to Power and Domination

1933

JANUARY

Hitler is appointed Chancellor of Germany.

MARCH:

Jews throughout Germany are attacked and beaten.

Dachau concentration camp is opened to house criminals against the state, this includes many Jews.

Government organizes one-day boycott of all Jewish shops.

Star of David is painted on all Jewish shop windows.

Thousands of books are burned in front of Berlin Opera House.

OCTOBER:

Placards appear at cafes, stadiums, shops and roads leading into towns which read: "Jews Not Wanted!"

1933 - 1935

Nazi aim is to eliminate all Jewish influence from every facet of German life, and therefore, encourage immigration to other countries. During those two years, 75,000 Jews leave Germany.

The remaining Jews in Germany are deprived of their professions and livelihood by boycott, decree or local pressure.

Reflections

The preparations for mass murder were made possible by Germany's military successes in the months following the invasion of Poland in 1939. ***But from the moment that Adolph Hitler had come to power in Germany in 1933, the devastating process had begun.*** *It was a process which depended upon the rousing of historic hatreds and ancient prejudice, and upon the cooperation or acquiescence of many different forces: of industry, science, and medicine, of the Civil Service and bureaucracy, and of the most modern mechanisms and channels of communication.*

Martin Gilbert, Author and Historian

There are some things that can only be done as long as they are not discussed, for once they are discussed they can no longer be done.

Raul Hilberg, Jewish Theologian

Be gracious to me, O LORD, for I am in distress; my eye wastes away from grief, my soul and body also. For my life is spent with sorrow, and my years with sighing; my strength fails because of my misery, and my bones waste away.

Psalm 31:9-10

Chapter 4 –
The Guilt and Shame of Silence

The "great silence" deafening in its denial of what was going on outside the safety net of her own home, continues to haunt Suzie, as she recalls day to day life under Nazi rule. The Belgians were very aware of what was happening to the Jews in their community, but silence prevailed as friends and neighbors slowly disappeared, never to be heard from again, the ensuing silence weaving a fabric of terror, horror and shame.

People didn't speak of or about their German occupiers, good or bad, as anything could be misconstrued to be anti-German and that usually meant deportation to work camps (as they were called) in the east. It was believed by most people that trouble could be avoided as long as they adhered to the dictates laid down by the Nazis.

Then one day the unthinkable happened. Two German soldiers marched into the cafe, not to eat, rather they were there to arrest Zanne's father, accusing him of being a Jew. She and her family stood, horrified, as her father was dragged from their home and shoved into a waiting truck. The days that followed were terror filled, as Zanne and her family waited for news, fully aware that in all probability they would never hear from him again. Expecting the worst, they were imprisoned by silence, their home becoming a tomb of unanswered questions.

Would she ever see her father again?

Was he being tortured?

Did the authorities know that her mother was part Jewish?

How would that knowledge affect the rest family?

How much Jewish blood qualified one for execution?

Miraculously, three days after her father's arrest, he was re-turned to them, relatively unscathed. The Germans could find no evidence of Jewish blood in his family history. [Had this happened later in the war, he probably would have been immediately sent to a death camp, as the question of innocence or guilt was no longer a part of the German legal system.]

A quiet celebration was held in thanksgiving for her father's safe return, but again silence prevailed. They knew that they were being closely watched and their constant companion was the lingering fear that her mother's lineage would be discovered, and that would mean the end for all of them.

Strangely enough, in spite of German thoroughness and meticulous record keeping, her mother's ancestry never came into question, but the fear of discovery held Zanne's family hostage until the liberation. A strange and unsettling silence became their only ally. Harboring her mother's secret filled Zanne with guilt and shame, as she continued to hear of others being taken from their homes, never to return.

Could her family have somehow helped those who were taken in the night?

What if it had been their mother brutally arrested and carried off?

What could one or two people do when faced with the Nazi menace?

Whom do you save?

Questions for which there are no right answers and that can never completely be resolved. Question's Suzie continues to wrestle with and peace eludes her.

A HISTORY -
The Deceitful Path to Dehumanization

September 15, 1935

Establishment of "Nuremberg Laws"

1. Citizenship can only belong to a national German or kindred blood (Jews defined as being not of German blood.)
2. Marriage between Jews and Germans is forbidden.

1938

German Jews deprived of rights of citizenship.

Buchenwald concentration camp is established.

In October German forces march into Czechoslovakia, reclaiming the Sudetenland for Germany. The 20,000 Jews living there flee to the east.

Three weeks later Hitler expels 18,000 Jews to the Polish border, which is done swiftly and with great brutality.

NOVEMBER 9

Stormtroopers break into tens of thousands of Jewish shops and homes, destroying what they can.

191 synagogues are set ablaze – the event being called "Kristallnacht," meaning the night of crystal, referring to the broken glass of the synagogue and shop windows.

Reflections

The cruelty of the Germans surpasses everything known in the annals of human history. Yet their greatest crime was not their cruelty, but their sophisticated system of planned destruction of the human status of their victims. Their terrible barbarous power over their helpless victims was not used to destroy them physically, but to degrade them to the extent of losing the last vestige of their self-respect.

The world has never known anything like that before. The cruelty of the Germans was different not only in degree from other forms of cruelty practiced by man against his fellow. Unique was their system of the planned dehumanization of their victims. It is the uniquely German crime against humanity, against the status of man. It is the crime most difficult to forgive or to forget.

Eliezer Berkovite, Jewish Theologian

On Roosters

I tell you, before the cock crows twice
  you will deny me thrice.
Not me, Lord, no . . . not me!

Let's face it . . . Jews are different.
why do they purposely set themselves apart?
They even look different.
Most Jews I know *do* have big noses.

Auschwitz wasn't
  my experience.
I am a Gentile.
I was an infant then.
It's past history.

Six million?
You've got to be kidding!
They couldn't have possibly
  have killed six million.
Maybe the Holocaust didn't even happen!

Not me, Lord, no . . . not me!
I will not deny you . . . .

Reflections

Why the Silence

As I researched and studied written materials concerning the Holocaust, I was overcome by the silence. It cried out to me, the silence of the people, whose neighbors were carried off in the middle of the night, the silence of the German bureaucrats, the silence of all the countries of the world, the silence that prevailed after the Holocaust, and in many ways still prevails today, and finally my own silence.

Is it true, I wonder, what the Jewish theologian Raul Hilberg says, 'There are some things that can be done only so long as they are not discussed, for if they are discussed they can no longer be done.'

If the Holocaust is not discussed, does it mean that it can happen again? Is that why the silence? Do we need the silence so we will forget and allow it to happen to reoccur? What form will it take next time? Who will be the victims; who will be the perpetrators; who will be the silent bystanders?

We all have choices to make in life. We all have moments of decision. Will we choose to speak out, to take action, or will we choose to be silent?

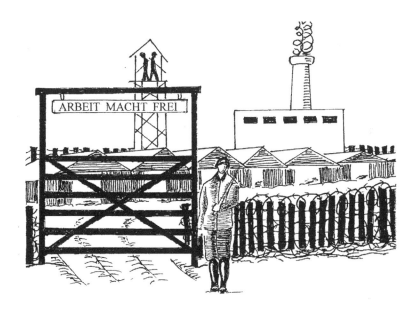

Deliver me, O LORD, from evildoers; protect me from those who are violent, who plan evil things in their minds and stir up wars continually.

Guard me, O LORD, from the hands of the wicked; protect me from the violent who have planned my downfall.

Psalm 140:1-2, 4

Chapter 5 – The Reality of War

It is a cacophony of noise, the intensity of which is far beyond the average human experience or imagination. It is the sound of wheels turning, screeching, whining and groaning as huge tanks, creaking in their might, move forward to meet the enemy. One explosion after another sounding as their huge cannons spew forth killing balls of fire containing shell fragments that penetrate and tear human flesh, inflicting pain, dismemberment and death.

It is the sound of repeated rifle fire, machine guns, bazookas and other instruments of terror and destruction that join together to create a roar as of hundreds of prowling lions stalking their prey. It is a noise that builds in intensity and terrifies the body and the soul, as it co-mingles with the screams and cries for help as shells find their victims and flesh is penetrated, torn, shattered, and demolished.

IT IS THE SOUND OF BATTLE!

There is another sound, however, given birth to by the roar of the killing machines, more terrifying than anything pre-imagined. It is a sound that envelopes the entire body, often rendering even the most elemental bodily functions beyond one's control. It is the sound of *fear*, manifested in one's body by the beating of one's own heart. It is a pounding in the ear, so loud and all encompassing that it almost drowns out the sounds of combat . . . *almost.*

Into this world of horror, noise, and death entered LaVern White, the young, innocent, patriotic farm boy from Grafton,

Iowa. He had spent sixteen months being trained for war, but nothing, not anything, had or could prepare him for the horror he encountered on the battlefield. Terror gripped his heart as he faced the enemy for the first time in November of 1944, at Metz, France, and the sound of his beating heart took control of his body. Three days, the fighting raged, LaVern experiencing being caught in the valley of the shadow of death. Destruction met him at every turn and there was no escape from the roar, the terrible, terrible roar.

Finally, the battle-weary German soldiers gave in to the fresh American forces, and the roar subsided. Much to LaVern's amazement he had survived his first encounter with the enemy. In those three days, he had learned one very important truth: in reality the war involved only two people . . . he and the soldier who fought alongside him, his buddy, who shared his foxhole. Together they had withstood the fire power aimed at them. He didn't care about the hundreds around him. His one purpose was to keep him and his buddy alive. It was just that simple and just that terrifying.

He had killed so that he would not be killed. How many bullets in his gun found their mark? How many had been wounded, maimed or paralyzed by the bullets expended by his weapon? These were the questions that plagued him, questions for which there were no answers. The pathway to insanity was paved with just such questions, and so consequently, he centered his thoughts on himself, his buddy and the two of them making it through the day. In order to survive the hell, which had now become his world, he reached deep into the center of his being, calling on the strength of character that had been molded by the prairie winds of Iowa.

He had to do what he had to do. The farm had taught him that great truth. When the winter storms swept across the fields bringing snow, ice, blinding wind and sub-zero temperatures, the animals still had to be watered and fed, and their stalls cleaned. It was frostbite inducing, back breaking work, but in order to survive . . . *it had to be done.* As a soldier in the United States Army, involved in the greatest conflict known to humankind in its history, LaVern knew what was expected of him and what he had to do. He was part of a vast armada sent to liberate Europe from the tyranny imposed upon its citizens by Nazi Germany. In the foxhole, however, he didn't think about the grand scheme of things or the politics involved. The war was he and his buddy somehow surviving so that one day he might return to the corn-fields of Iowa and again feel God's breath in the ever changing prairie winds . . . and so he killed.

He did what his country asked of him because he was a true patriot. In the midst of the insanity of war, deep in the core of his being, he knew that his participation in this noble cause would help to ensure the freedom of generations to come . . . and so he killed.

In those three terror-filled days, his whole world view had been altered, his innocence lost forever and the horror and reality of war had shaken the very foundations of his being. Overnight he became a man, carrying the weight of the world upon his shoulders. He believed that he was ready as he would ever be for the task at hand. This confidence was soon to be tested.

To this day, LaVern insists that this narrative makes him sound like a hero. "I am no hero," he states with typical humility. "I just did what I had to do."

LaVern's anti-aircraft unit, armed with 40-millimeter and quad 50 caliber machine guns, was attached to the 87th Infantry Division. The division, a part of General Patton's Third Army, sprinted across France toward Germany at breakneck speed. "He was hard-headed and had a very bad temper," recalled LaVern, in speaking about General Patton. "But he sure knew how to fight Germans. He never let up, not giving them any time to regroup. He just kept pounding away."

One day LaVern found himself standing right next to Patton. "It made me feel scared, being that close to such a powerful man. His whole being exuded energy that was positively contagious. He was a very difficult person, with a displeasing personality, but I knew I was standing next to greatness. It was quite humbling."

The Third Army's advance reached the Siegfried Line (France's ineffective defense front to Germany) in December, 1944. The Germans were thought to be on their heels and retreating back to the homeland, but they were not about to give up so easily. They hit the US forces with everything they had in a last gasp counter-attack that began in the Ardennes on the German-Belgium border, and came to be known in the annals of military history as the "The Battle of the Bulge." The Germans were running low on gasoline and they were desperate to reach and take over the large US fuel dumps located in Belgium.

The Allies response to the attack was blunted by foul weather that grounded aircraft and winter conditions that made surviving, much less fighting, an ordeal.

Reinforcements were directed to the Bastogne area, where the fighting was the most fierce and LaVern's anti-aircraft outfit was ordered to help slow down the German advance.

"Our direct fire aimed at the German ground force was devastating, but we were no match for the Tiger tanks," he shares. "They were impenetrable. They just kept coming and coming, huge armored machines killing and destroying everything in their path."

It was very evident that LaVern's outfit was meant to be sacrificed in the process. The US strategy was to slow the Germans down, no matter the cost so that Allied air power could be thrown into the fray. The weather cleared more quickly than expected and LaVern's unit was spared becoming involved in what would have likely been a bloody battle to the death.

"We lucked out," he says, with an indescribable expression on his face, a face now hidden by emotions and memories that at times are too difficult to share.

As he had been at the forefront of two large and significant battles, LaVern thought he had witnessed the ultimate depths of human depravity. However, as the 87th Infantry crossed the Rhine River and headed into Germany early in 1945, he was ushered into a world of horror and deprivation, beyond anything he could have imagined.

As he speaks of it, tears form, falling softly down his cheeks, his speech slows, and a quietness envelops him. From the depths of his Iowa being, he whispers, "It was just too much . . . it was just too much."

A HISTORY -
Sinking Into The Abyss

1939

JANUARY 30:

Speaking in Berlin, Hitler declares that in the event of war. "The result will not be the bolshevization of the earth, and thus the victory of the Jewry, but the annihilation of the Jewish race in Europe."

SEPTEMBER:

Germany invades Poland.

Britain and France declare war on Germany.

Mass killings of Poles, 5,000 Jews killed by German troops in Poland.

Adolf Eichmann is put in charge of "Jewish Resettlement."

NOVEMBER 19

Order for the removal of all Jews from western Poland; Germans need the "Lebensraum" (Living space).

Where Jews are allowed to live they experience daily raids by German officers demanding money, jewels, goods, and food. Women were searched intimately for such items.

Germany seeks world domination.

1940

War in the west and terror in the east.

With no warning German troops occupy, Norway, Holland and France, and Belgium.

MAY 25:

Confident in a speedy German victory, Reich's Fuhrer, Himmler, sends the following note to Hitler in which he refers to the world as he would like it to be after the war, *"I hope the concept of the Jew will have completely disappeared from Europe."*

Jews no longer allowed to immigrate.

140,000 non-German Jews are trapped behind German lines and subject to German laws.

JUNE:

The establishment of Auschwitz concentration camp.

The establishment of the Warsaw Ghetto, many cities follow their example, creating separate living areas for the Jews, who were not allowed to leave the ghetto.

Jews in ghettos existing on a sub-poverty level, in which living conditions were deplorable.

How long, O LORD? Will you forget me forever? How long will you hide your face from me?

How long must I bear pain in my soul, and have sorrow in my heart all day long? How long shall my enemy be exalted over me?

Psalm 13:1-2

Chapter 6 –
Resistance, Frustration, and Weariness

In Webster's Dictionary the word *"fear"* is defined as a feeling of dread; alarm; or fright. It is anxious concern or worry, cause for alarm; danger.

Fear, dread, fright, alarm, dismay, consternation, panic, terror and horror are all synonyms of the word, *"fear."*

Fear is the most general term used for all of the above.

Dread emphasizes anxiety.

Alarm suggests the surprise and agitation excited by imminent or unexpected danger.

Dismay implies deprivation of spirit, courage, or initiative, especially by an alarming **prospect**.

Consternation heightens the implication of confusion.

Panic is overmastering and unreasoning, often groundless fear or fright.

Terror suggests the extremity of consternation or (often violent) dread.

Horror adds the implication of shuddering abhorrence.

By 1944, German occupation forces had perfected the use of fear in governing the populace in the countries that had invaded and called their "own." With no regard for the dignity of their fellow human beings, they ruled by intimidation, threats, and un-explained and sudden arrests.

Zanne and her family and their neighbors lived in constant fear. While little was ever said out loud about what went on in the camps, it was general knowledge that they existed and horrific things, unimaginable in scope, transpired there. It was known that to be arrested and put on one of the transports meant certain death. (The transports were trains made up of cattle cars, in which people were stuffed and where there was standing room only. It was usually a two to three-day trip and many did not survive.)

As the war progressed it became more and more difficult for people to stand by and witness the atrocities being committed on a daily basis, and do nothing in retaliation. Two of Zanne's brothers along with countless other Belgians joined the Resis-tance, becoming British agents and soon were involved in a clan-destine operation that put the entire family at risk.

In a yard behind the cafe, they raised and trained doves to act as carrier pigeons. The birds carried vital messages back and forth across the English Channel and the information supplied by the small fowl proved to be crucial for Ally decision-making, es-pecially in regards to D-Day. While the danger was real and the accompanying fear almost intolerable, they welcomed the oppor-tunity to finally be doing something that might help to rid the world of the Nazi menace.

Zanne was always amazed that those little birds could find their way home, with their encoded messages secure and encased in a metal band around one leg. Surprisingly, the Gestapo never suspected a thing. Had they been pigeons rather than doves, questions might have been raised, but they appeared to be just plain and harmless birds. Zanne's brothers and their trained carri-ers continued to play an active role in the Resistance until the war's end.

A HISTORY -
The Beginning of the End for Adolf Hitler

1941

Germany breaks peace agreement with Russia and German troops invade Russia, enforcing a parched earth policy [burning everything in their wake so that the Russian citizens would have nothing to eat or the ability to sustain life] as they marched towards Stalingrad.

1942 - 1943

Field Marshal Rommel's Africa Korps defeated by the Allies.

German soldiers, numbering 91,000 including twenty-four generals are driven west, out of Stalingrad, hundreds of miles by an onslaught of Russian troops.

The Germans in full retreat are half starved, suffering from frostbite, and many are wounded. All of them are dazed and broken, hobbling over ice and snow, ill-clad for winter weather, experiencing their parched earth policy first hand.

They will now experience the horrors which their armed forces had inflicted on others.

William L. Shirer, in his book, *The Rise and Fall of the Third Reich,* states it so well:

"Finally, in the snows of Stalingrad and in the burning sands of the North African desert, a great and terrible Nazi dream was destroyed."

IT IS THE BEGINNING OF THE END

My God, my God, why have you forsaken me? Why are you so far from helping me, from the words of my groanings?

O my god, I cry by day, but you do not answer, and by night, but find no rest.

Psalm 22:1-2

Chapter 7 – Buchenwald

There are things of which you can speak and there are things that are unspeakable. They are beyond the scope of the human vocabulary, for there are no words that can adequately express what one has seen and heard.

Then there are words, however, that cry out volumes, that by themselves conjure up such vivid images, that no other word is necessary.

Treblinka

Bergen-Belsen

Auschwitz

BUCHENWALD

The names of four of the most infamous death camps built and operated by Nazi Germany; each word tells its own story; one word that bespeaks of the suffering of millions. Just one of these names can create images of gallows, whipping posts, gas chambers, belching furnaces, plumes of black smoke spewing out of giant smokestacks and a stench that permeates all. It is the stench of rotting flesh being turned to ash by the furnaces of the crematorium, "Ashes to ashes, dust to dust, earth to earth." It is a smell that climbs into one's nasal cavities and resides there, seemingly forever, reminding one of things done to fellow human beings that are unspeakable.

As Patton's army left Belgium, fighting their way across France and finally penetrating "The Fatherland," it was the stench that first alerted the troops, one of them being LaVern White, that something was not right. As they moved forward, the sky became darker and darker and yet not a cloud could be seen. It became apparent that it was smoke that was darkening the sky, and as the troops continued on there was an accompanying stench which seemed to envelop them. Soon there loomed before them a huge compound surrounded by barbwire and watched over by guard towers strategically placed. As far as the eye could see, stretched rows and rows of barrack-like buildings. Rising above the whole area were huge smokestacks spewing forth the black smoke that continued to darken the sky.

Over the entrance to the compound were the words, "Arbeit Macht Frei" (Work Makes One Free). Into the hell of the Buchenwald Concentration camp walked the Iowa farm boy, his life to be forever altered by the horrors he would encounter in the ensuing moments.

"The Germans had obviously left in a hurry, their work not yet completed," says LaVern, quietly. "There were bodies everywhere, some alive, but most of them dead or dying. Bodies were stacked like cordwood on large flatbed wagons. Others were piled up in huge trenches, all naked and lying on top of each other. It appeared that they had been thrown in like so much garbage. Some of those just lying on the ground were partially dressed in prison blue and white stripped material. Some had been shot, while others looked like they had just dropped dead from "natural causes."

"We went into one of the barrack-like buildings," LaVern continued. "The stench seemed to follow us wherever we went. It was unbearable. It was very dark and at first we couldn't see much. As our eyes grew accustomed to the dimness we could see rows and rows of bunks that were full of skeletons. As we drew closer the skeletons began to move, moan and clatter, making strange rattling sounds. We suddenly realized they were not skeletons but live people, skeletons with skin on them. They held out their hands, begging, I guess, for food. I could not understand what they were saying. I couldn't take it any longer. I turned and ran out of the building gasping for air, but there was no relief . . . just the stench. We were at the camp an hour and then ordered to move out. In that hour, my life view was forever altered. How can a human being do this to another human being, I asked myself over and over. I still ask that question. It was just too much . . . it was just too much," he whispers as he retreats into silence, tears streaming down his face.

It was just too much . . . it was just too much.

Reflections on Buchenwald

One of the most prominent features in the camp was the smokestack from the crematory. There was never a time when it wasn't belching black smoke, and never a time when there wasn't an odor in the camp easily identified with the crematory.

The corpse carriers were one of the more active working teams in Buchenwald. From 800 to 2,000 people died every day. We estimated that if you were Norwegian, Dutch, Danish, you might survive. If you were Belgian or French, your chances were slightly poorer. If you were Czechoslovakian or Hungarian, they were even poorer. As a Polish prisoner, you had a life expectancy of three weeks. The Jews of course, were a totally separate category, brought into Buchenwald for the express purpose of being exterminated.

As the war approached its end in the spring of 1945, we hardly got any food at all. I was convinced I wouldn't survive because we were all thinking "The Germans are not going to let us get out and tell about it."

A Holocaust Survivor

Auschwitz

Auschwitz was not my experience;
I am an American,
I am white
I am intelligent,
I am gifted.
I am the perfect "Aryan,"

BUT -----

I love
I hate
I think
I feel
I laugh
I know pain
I bleed
I cry,

I am a human being!

It is my experience!

The Valley of Dry Bones

The hand of the Lord came upon me and he brought me out by the spirit of the Lord and set me down in the middle of a valley; it was full of bones. He led me all around them; there very many lying in the valley, and they were very dry. He said to me, "Mortal, can these bones live?" I answered, "O Lord God, you know."

Then he said to me, "Prophesy to these bones, and say to them: O dry bones, hear the word of the Lord. Thus says the Lord God to these bones; I will cause breath to enter you, and you shall live. I will lay sinews on you, and cause flesh to come upon you, and cover you with skin, and put breath in you, and you shall live; and you shall know that I am the LORD."

So I prophesied as I had been commanded; and as I prophesied, suddenly there was a noise, a rattling, and the bones came together, bone to its bone. I looked, and there were sinews on them, and flesh had come upon them, and skin had come upon them; but there was no breath in them. Then he said to me, "Prophesy to the breath, prophesy, mortal, and say to the breath; Thus says the Lord God; Come from the four winds, O breath, and breathe upon these slain, that they might live." I prophesied as he commanded me and the breath came into them; and they lived, and stood on their feet, a vast multitude.

Then he said to me, "Mortal, these bones are the whole house of Israel. They say, 'Our bones are dried up, and our hope is lost; we are cut off completely.' Therefore prophesy, and say to them, Thus says the Lord God; I am going to open your graves, and bring you up from your graves, O my people; and I will bring you back to the land of Israel. And you shall know that I am the Lord, when I open your graves and bring you up from your graves, O my people. I will put my spirit within you, and you shall live, and I will place you on your own soil; then you shall know that I the LORD, have spoken and will act," says the Lord.

Ezekiel 37

A HISTORY -
The Final Solution

The Wannsee Conference
January 20, 1942

What: A gathering of the fifteen highest officials of the German Government.

Where: Wannsee, a quiet suburb of Berlin.

Why:

1. To discuss "the final solution" to the Jewish problem, the elimination of the Jewish race in Europe.

2. Needed to clean up fundamental problems involved in logistics so that the "final solution" could at last be realized. This meant ending the lives of *eleven million people.*

Conclusions:

1. All Jews were to be transported by rail to the conquered East.

2. If they survived the transport they were to be worked to death.

3. The tough who survived transport and work details were to eventually be gassed.

4. Children, the elderly, infirmed and those disabled in any way were to be immediately sent to the gas chamber upon arrival at the camp.

Reflections

The phrase, "Final Solution," had a deeper, more significant meaning. In Himmler's words, the Jewish problem would never have to be solved again. Definitions, expropriations, and concentrations can be undone. Killings are irreversible. Hence, they gave to the destruction process its quality of historical finality.

The killing of Jews was regarded as historical necessity. The soldier had to "understand" this.

Raul Hilberg, Jewish Theologian

The Holocaust was not a throwback to medieval torture or archaic barbarism but a thoroughly modern expression of bureaucratic organization, industrial management, scientific achievement, and technological sophistication.

Elie Wiesel, Holocaust Survivor and Nobel Prize-winning advocate for Peace

Since the fourth century, there have been three anti-Jewish policies:

300 AD *You can no longer live among us as Jews, so convert.*

1500 AD *You can no longer live among us.*

1942 AD *You can no longer live.*

Raul Hilberg, Jewish Theologian

Trains

Clickety-clack, clickety-clack,
Oh, how I love to ride the train.

The haunting sound of the whistle,
Oh, how I love to ride the train.

Beautiful snow-capped mountains speeding by,
Oh, how I love to ride the train.

Wonderful food and tables set with linens and flowers,
Oh, how I love to ride the train.

But, I have heard...
There were other trains...

Clickety-clack, clickety clack,
A train carrying the promise of death.

A whistle shrieking, "Out of the way, out of the way!"
A train carrying the promise of death.

Nothing but darkness and cries for help,
A train carrying the promise of death.

Oh, how I love to ride the train.
NO . . . NO . . . NOT THIS TRAIN!

I will extol you, O LORD, for you have drawn me up, and did not let my foes rejoice over me.

O LORD, my God, I cried to you for help, and you healed me.

Psalm 30:1-2

Chapter 8 – Liberation

The Belgians began to wonder if the war would ever come to an end. In spite of all their underground efforts to rid their country of the German occupying forces, the Nazis remained entrenched. The war dragged on and on, and the bombings continued, both day and night.

"Would the killing ever stop?" wondered Zanne.

"First you would hear the drone of the plane's engines and then the screaming of the bombs falling from the sky, hitting their targets with huge explosive sounds," says Suzie, as she continues to talk about the raids that never stopped.

"It seemed like one continuous attack," she states, as she tries to explain the horror of those days, and the experiences she cannot get past. The more she talks about it, the quieter she becomes, her voice just a whisper.

"It was awful, terrifying!"

The factories that surrounded her parent's cafe were prime targets for both the Allies and the Germans because they produced coal products, phosphorus, and gasoline, all of which were needed in the war effort on both sides. To this day, her dreams continue to be filled with screams and the wailing of the injured and dying. She can still hear, in her mind's eye, the sobbing that took hold of the survivors who had to dig loved ones out from under the rubble and destruction left in the wake of the falling bombs.

"I will never get over it . . . *never*," she murmurs softly, sharing that the nightmares those images produce seem to be worse and more frequent as she grows older.

One incident, in particular, stands out in her memory, as is if it had happened only yesterday, and yet it has been over sixty years since it occurred. Two days before the liberating American army reached Zanne's town, the BBC announced that there would be an Allied bombing raid the next day, aimed at the factories located near their cafe. (The *British Broadcasting Company* kept Europeans who possessed "forbidden" radios informed on a daily basis, of the progress of the Allies in their attempt to liberate Western Europe from Nazi domination. The BBC also broadcast coded messages to the resistance and those British agents working behind enemy lines.)

It was supposed to be a pinpoint bombing. Bombs were to be dropped only on specifically designated targets. But to be sure that the local citizenry did not come to any great harm, they were advised to go to places of relative safety until the raid was over. Zanne and her family took refuge in a nearby town where one of her brothers and his family lived. Unfortunately, that community was mistakenly bombed, devastating most of the town and many people were grievously injured.

After the raid, Zanne discovered her sister-in-law's sister amidst the rubble that surrounded them, alive, but both of her legs had been blown off. She was conscious and alert and asked Zanne to look for her parents. After a long and difficult search, she finally found the dismembered bodies of the girl's parents and then had to disclose the sorrowful news to this young girl, now facing life without her legs and her parents.

More horror awaited them upon their return to Reime-Eerwalde. To their dismay, they discovered that much of the city had been flattened by the bombing. Of the structures left standing, many were badly damaged. Miraculously, their home/cafe had escaped the devastation that befell the buildings around them. It had been hit, but was still standing, and the repairs that were needed appeared to be well within the skill level of Zanne's brothers.

"What more can happen," cried Zanne."What more can they do to us?" "How much more can we endure?"

Two days later into the midst of the rubble, destruction, and horror marched the liberating American army and one very special soldier, LaVern White, of Grafton, Iowa.

Little did Zanne know on that bright and beautiful morning that she would meet, fall in love and marry one of those handsome American GI's marching by her family's cafe. Being swept away by the heightened emotions that only occur in the very young and in the unusual circumstances in which they found themselves, Zanne's life journey would be forever changed.

The day would come when she would leave the Old World for the New, crossing the broad expanse of the Atlantic Ocean to America, the land of promised dreams.

A HISTORY -
The Twilight of the Gods

1944

JUNE 6 – D-DAY

The Allied invasion of Europe at Normandy.

1944 - 1945

The trains with cattle cars filled with Jews continue to roll eastward.

DECEMBER, 1944

The Battle of the Bulge – Germany's last great offensive. The German troops are badly beaten and forced to retreat.

1945

The Allies invade Germany and begin to liberate concentration camp inmates.

The conditions found in the camps are horrible beyond words.

MAY 2

Hitler commits suicide.

MAY 9

Germany surrenders to the Allies.

Reflections

Every survivor of the Holocaust faces the past and confronts the future with a burden which those who did not go through the torment, cannot measure. "I may bear indelible scars in body and soul," Cordilia Edvardson *has written, "but I don't intend to reveal them to the world – least of all to the Germans. That is the pride of the survivor. Hitler is dead –* **but I am alive!"**

Cordilia Edvardson, Holocaust Survivor, German-born Swedish Journalist and Author

The LORD sets the prisoners free; the LORD opens the eyes of the blind.

The LORD lifts up those who are bowed down; the LORD loves the righteous.

The LORD watches over the strangers; he upholds the orphan and the widow, but the way of the wicked he brings to ruin.

Psalm 146:7b-9

O give thanks to the LORD, for he is good and his steadfast love endures forever.

Psalm 136:1

Chapter 9 – The Wonder of Spring

The war in Europe was over and all of creation was rejoicing. April showers had brought May flowers and everywhere little, colorful buds were emerging; daffodils, tulips, crocuses, and tiny violets, showing up in the small patches of grass that had survived the brutality of battle. And of course, there were dandelions, God's wonderful reminder of resurrection. Every year they burst forth, as a golden sea of color, splashed upon the vivid green of new spring grass. They are trampled, run over and poisoned, but still they return, a new creation each spring. Their sunny faces seem to say, "Rejoice, *Rejoice!* Spring is here, **Spring is here!**

Zanne's family had worked night and day to repair the damage done to their cafe in the last air raid and it was now open for business. It soon became very popular with the Allied soldiers stationed at nearby bases. The food was good, the liquor plentiful and a warm welcome always awaited them. Zanne was intrigued by the different national personalities, so readily apparent. The British men were polite, quiet, reserved and very serious, while the Canadians were rude and obnoxious. The Americans - well, they were just plain fun to be around. They exuded an aura of acceptance, confidence, and generosity.

"Oh," thought Zanne. "America must be a wonderful country." All she really knew about it, she had learned from the movies. Films usually depicted a magical place, where everyone was rich, happy and possessed luxuries beyond belief. It was truly the land of "milk and honey," at least that was Hollywood's claim.

————————————

The war was over! It was May, and the spring flowers were emerging, poking their little buds through every crack and crevice they could find. Many were different from the Iowa prairie flowers with which LaVern was familiar, but that did not matter. They were beautiful, fresh and announced the promise of new life. Being raised on a farm, he knew that spring was the most important season in the year. If the crop is not planted during the window of time God gives, there is risk of no or little income for that year. Consequently, the farmer has to be astutely aware of the signs that spring is just around the corner.

The type of flower that blooms, gives him hints about the ground temperature. If the ground is not fit [meaning not warm enough] the seeds will not germinate. In other words, if they sit too long in cold, damp soil, the harvest will be minimal. His thoughts about spring led him to the dandelion, the flower that knows no borders, the survivor of all things. He often thought that he and his buddy were like the dandelions.

They had taken many beatings, fought long and hard and had experienced what no one should experience and see, and they had survived to greet another spring. They had walked through the valley of the shadow of death and were now rejoicing in the green pastures of peace.

LaVern's unit was stationed at a base in Holland just across the Belgian border from Rieme-Ertvelde, Zanne's hometown. He was assigned to the base's motor pool as a truck driver. His job was to load food and supplies onto his vehicle and take them to a DP (displaced persons) camp in the south of France. It was usually a four-day trip.

He hated his job because the facility was filled with concentration camp survivors and other people left homeless by the war. The people seemed to carry with them the terrible stench he had experienced at Buchenwald. The stench took root in the truck's cab, growing in intensity with each trip, permeating everything. "Would he ever be free of it?" he wondered.

His route took him through the heart of Reime-Etwalde. He was fascinated by the Belgian buildings, greatly appreciating the architecture. He marveled at how well they were maintained, especially considering all the bombing raids they had experienced.

LaVern was used to the vastness of the Iowa prairie, wide open spaces and being able to see forever, consequently he was struck by the density of the population in Belgian communities. He was amazed at how close all the buildings were to each other, some even sharing a common wall. It made for a completely different lifestyle from what he had always known. He missed the peace and quiet of the cornfields and the sight of the lightening bugs keeping watch over the crops by night.

[The lightning bugs, also called fireflies, are small flying insects native to the Midwest that appear on the scene in mid-summer, dispelling the darkness of the night. When they sit on a stalk of grain, they momentarily emit a very bright light. It is truly an awesome sight to see a bean field full of their blinking lights. It holds one captive in awe and wonder, again contemplating the miracle of God's creation.]

Signs of spring were everywhere, despite the town being a densely populated urban area. Most of the buildings boasted window boxes, in which sprouting plants could be seen and blades of bright green grass were poking their way up through the spaces between the cobblestones on the streets he traveled.

He wondered if his dad had started to plant corn. It was the right time.

"Was the ground fit?" he wondered.

As he was pondering spring and how it revealed itself, something caught his eye. He swiftly turned his head, almost driving off the road in order to get a better look. Standing on the corner was the most beautiful girl he had ever seen. There she stood, a vision of such loveliness that it took his breath away. Her sparkling eyes seemed to be beckoning him to have a closer look.

"One could lose himself in those eyes," he thought as he fought to gain control of the truck and his emotions. His heart was pounding, his palms were sweaty and he felt as though he had been struck by lightning.

"Who is she?" he wondered. "Will I ever see here again? I must see her again, I must."

The next time he made the trip to the DP camp, and thus going through Rieme-Ertvelde, he was so nervous, *so* nervous he could barely keep control of the steering wheel.

"Was it just a dream? Did I really see her, or was it my imagination running wild? Was she only a vision?" Such were LaVern's thoughts as he left the base with another load of supplies for the DP camp. He was so anxious about the possibility of seeing her again that he didn't even think about the stench that would be awaiting him at his destination.

As he approached *the corner*, he shifted into low gear, so he could pass by slowly.

And there she was! Exactly where she had been before, looking more lovely than he had remembered. Her beautiful eyes were dancing, and her porcelain-like face, was framed with beautiful brown hair. He summoned up all of the Iowa courage he could muster, rolled down the cab window and *waved*.

"Oh my gosh," he thought. "Now I've done it. She probably thinks I am a brash American on the make. Why, oh why did I do that? I don't even know her. Boy, that was a dumb thing to do."

He looked again, and there she was waving to him, with a shy smile lighting up her face and making her beautiful eyes dance in excitement.

A HISTORY -
The Holocaust

1939 - 1945:

Of the eight million Jews living in Europe, six million were exterminated by the Nazis.

Jews alone were marked to be destroyed in their entirety: every Jewish man, woman, and child, *so that there would be no Jewish life left in Europe.*

The Nazis also killed many millions of non-Jewish civilians in Germany and the countries they occupied, shooting them in cold blood, citizens that had not taken part in any military action. Others killed under Nazi rule were:

1. A quarter of a million Gypsies.

2. Tens of thousands of homosexuals.

3. Tens of thousands of 'mental defectives.'

4. Several million Soviet prisoners of war.

Simply to survive was a victory of the human spirit.

The LORD has heard my supplication, the LORD accepts my prayer.

All my enemies shall be ashamed and struck with terror; they shall turn back, and in a moment be put to shame.

Psalm 6:9-10

Chapter 10 – When the Love Bug Bites, It Really Bites Hard

When the Love Bug Bites, It Really Bites Hard
LaVern White

LaVern White was in love, wildly, hopelessly in love. It was that once in a lifetime happening that few people rarely experience. He was swept away by emotions previously unknown to him and his whole world was now centered around the girl with the beautiful eyes. He couldn't explain it. It made no sense. He didn't even know her name, but he knew that they would be together forever; of that there was no doubt in his mind.

He had been bitten by the love bug and there was no turning back. Night and day he dreamed about the girl with the beautiful eyes, standing on the street corner, smiling and waving to him! That heavenly porcelain like face seemed to be always in front of him, invading his being to the very depth of his soul.

He had to do something. No longer was he satisfied with the tentative waves that had ensued in the days following his initial move. On his next trip to the DP camp, he purposely slowed his vehicle down as he approached "their corner." There she was. Not taking the time to second guess his actions, he stopped the truck and getting out of the cab, he walked across the street to where she stood.

His sudden action startled her and she turned to run from him. "No, no," cried LaVern. "Don't run away."

Even though she was unable to understand what he was saying [she did not speak English and he didn't know Flemish] she stopped, turned around, taking him in with those incredible eyes and he was lost *forever*!

"What is your name?" he asked.

Realizing that she might not understand him, he followed with, "My name is LaVern," repeating it a second time and pointing to himself.

She stood there, quietly contemplating what he had just said, and then her eyes started to sparkle and she said in a hushed voice, "Suzanne . . . Suzanne."

He repeated her name over and over, "Suzanne . . . Suzanne."

She started to shake her head, however, saying "no . . . no." Somehow she then managed to tell him that while her given name was indeed Suzanne, all of her family and close friends called her "Zanne."

At that point she turned, and before he could stop her, she ran from him, disappearing down one of the narrow cobblestone streets, adjacent to where he was standing.

He realized that he was already quite late with his delivery, and therefore, did not dare take the time to run after her. As he drove slowly away, leaving Rieme-Ertvelde behind him, he swore to himself that he would return and comb the entire town if necessary, in order to find her.

The following Saturday, with his weekend pass in hand and his buddy at his side he returned to the factory town that was home to Zanne, with the sole purpose of finding her.

His buddy thought he was nuts.

"How are you going to locate her in a town of 50,000 people?" he asked LaVern. "It's just not possible. You are certifiably nuts, nuts, nuts!" He exclaimed.

LaVern was not to be dissuaded, however, and so they began the search, starting in the central part of the business district, going from one store to the other, looking for anything that might lead him to Zanne.

As they passed a photographer's shop, LaVern suddenly stopped. He could not believe his eyes. There amidst other photos on display that showed the work of the owner was a beautiful photograph of Zanne.

"There she is," he shouted to his friend." That's Zanne!" pointing to her picture. "Isn't she the most beautiful girl you have ever seen? I told you we would find her. I told you, and you thought I was nuts. Isn't she beautiful? Well, say something!"

His buddy was dumbstruck. "She is incredibly beautiful," he thought to himself, so beautiful that he was left speechless. All week he had been teasing LaVern about her, certain that his words of adoration were over exaggerated. No one girl could possibly be that pretty. Well . . . he had been wrong.

"I don't know what to say, LaVern. She is all you said she is, and more!"

LaVern barely heard him, however, as he was already in the shop looking for the owner. As the man approached the counter, LaVern, without any greeting of any kind, asked, "Who is that girl in the window?"

"Oh, you Americans," the man replied in quite good English. "You are always so brash and think that the whole world belongs to you. What girl? There are many pictures on display in my window and besides, I can not divulge the names of my customers."

LaVern was taken aback by the rudeness of the shop owner and at first didn't know what to say or do. He took a moment to get hold of his emotions and then, in a calm voice said, "Come, I will show you the picture I am talking about."

"Oh, alright," muttered the man as he followed LaVern out the door of his shop.

"That's the picture, right there," LaVern exclaimed as he pointed to Zanne's photograph.

"Ah," said the man, with a sneer. "She is a beauty, isn't she'? No wonder you are interested in her. I can't give you her name."

"Why not?" asked LaVern, starting to get upset.

"Company rules," the man replied.

"What company?" asked LaVern,

"Mine," the photographer smugly answered.

"Alright then, I will buy the picture and find her myself," stated LaVern.

"It's not for sale."

"What do you mean, it is not for sale?"

"Just what I said, it is not for sale. You are not the only one that her picture has brought into my shop. Many have commented on what a fine photographer I must be to have produced such a beautiful photograph," he stated in a way that made LaVern boil.

Trying to keep his temper under control, LaVern asked in a quiet voice, "How much do you want?"

After much haggling, the photographer finally gave in and they settled on a price in much coveted American dollars. The picture now belonged to LaVern. [That picture still sits on LaVern's desk, her beauty immortalized, a reminder of those spring days when they were in love and anything was possible.]

As he was going out the door of the shop, the owner called out, "There is a cafe around the corner, not too far from here, you might try looking there."

Reflections on the Holocaust

Those who forget history are condemned to repeat it. The Holocaust reveals a potential pathology at the heart of western civilization together with the frightening consequences of total exercise of power. Remembering can instill caution, fortify restraint, and protect against future evil or indifference. The sense of outrage in the face of the Holocaust expressed in the declaration, "Never Again," neither to the Jewish people nor to any other people, must be informed by an understanding of what happened and why.

**Elie Wiesel, Holocaust Survivor and
Nobel Prize-winning advocate for Peace**

Make me to know your ways, O LORD; teach me your paths. Lead me in your truth, and teach me, for you are the God of my salvation; for you I wait all day long.

Be mindful of your mercy, O LORD, and of your steadfast love, for they have been from of old...according to your steadfast love remember me, for your goodness' sake, O LORD!

Psalm 25:4-7

Chapter 11 – Getting to Know You

The cafe was full of contented people, making happy sounds. It was the kind of ambiance that comes with a good meal, fine wine, and congenial conversation. It was the sound Zanne's family loved to hear because it meant people were pleased with the food and all that went with it and in all likelihood would return another day.

They were still getting used to their new Saturday crowd which consisted mostly of soldiers from the nearby Allied bases, happily putting their weekend passes to good use and spending *lots* of money. Monday through Friday, most of the cafe's trade came from the workers in the surrounding factories. However since the factories were closed on weekends Saturdays and Sundays were usually quiet. All that had changed when the Allies came to town. Now Saturday and Sunday were the busiest and most hectic days of the week.

"Whew, things must move quickly in America," thought Zanne, as she mopped her brow, scurrying from one table to the next, trying to keep up with all the orders.

Most of the soldiers that day were Americans, and they did not like to wait. They wanted their food, **now!**

Unfortunately, the cafe's kitchen was not set up for fast food service and consequently impatience often raised its head in the form of anger and frustration. Zanne usually kept her customers content by quickly filling their drink orders, and encouraging them to have seconds while they waited.

It had only been a few days since her first encounter with the very handsome young American soldier, but he was all she could think about and it was interfering with her efficiency as a waitress. Periodically her mother would poke her head out of the kitchen door to see what was going on with Zanne. Normally she was very quick in submitting orders, but on this particular day she was moving at a snail's pace. Every time her mother looked into the dining room, there Zanne would be, just standing in one spot, staring off into space. Her mother would shake her head and quietly remind Zanne that she had a job to do, and she had better get with it.

"I don't know what has gotten into Zanne, lately," she said to her husband that evening. "All she does is stand around with this far away look on her face. If I didn't know better, I would think she is in love!"

"Maybe she is," replied her father, who was the practical one in the family.

"Oh, don't be ridiculous. Surely we would know if something was going on, mothers sense these things, you know, besides, when does she have the time to have a boyfriend? We keep her far too busy in the cafe for her to be fooling around."

"Just mark my words," said her father, grinning from ear to ear, "I think love is in the air."

"Humph," snorted her mother. "A lot you know about young girls in love!"

Zanne's father was closer to the truth than her mother realized. Perhaps she wasn't in love, for she really didn't know him, but that good looking American was a constant presence in her daydreams.

It had all started so innocently. She was going on an errand for her mother and had stopped at the corner to wait for traffic to let up so she could cross the street. As she stood there an American army truck came by and as it passed her, it careened to one side almost going off the road.

The driver slammed on the breaks and thus missed ending up on the sidewalk. She could see that he had been looking at her, rather than paying attention to the road.

She could not help but smile at his "foolishness" and that made him grin in return.

"He sure is a handsome hunk," thought Zanne. And then he and his truck were gone, rumbling down the street and away from her.

She could not get his face and that cute grin out of her mind. "I wonder if he makes that trip often," she contemplated. She had noticed that he was driving what looked to be some kind of a delivery truck which meant he might travel that route through her town on a regular basis. She managed to think of other reasons to be gone about the same time every morning. She would leave the cafe and run to the corner.

There she would stand, hoping, hope against hope that he might pass that way again. For days, there was no soldier or truck to be seen. And then, one morning, when she was just about to give up any hope at all, she heard the rumbling sound of a truck on the cobblestone street, coming her way. Much to her joy it was *her* soldier, that American with the cute smile.

As he drew closer to where she was standing he slowed his vehicle and to her amazement rolled down the cab window and waved. Without even thinking she raised her hand and returned his wave.

In the days that followed she managed to be at "their corner," returning his waves with more and more enthusiasm. And then, one morning as he came down the street, instead of slowing down and waving, he brought the truck to a complete stop, got out of the cab and walked over to where she was standing.

"Now what have I done?" thought Zanne. She was suddenly frightened. She didn't know this man at all and yet she had been leading him on and now here he was standing right in front of her. As she quickly turned to run he said to her, "No, don't run away, no . . . please."

She did not speak English, but "no" was a universal word and she had learned what "please" meant from English speaking soldiers who frequented the cafe. She turned around and looked at him, trying to comprehend what was he was saying.

She could tell that he was asking her a question, but she did not recognize the words he was using.

He saw her confusion and he started to point to himself, saying, "LaVern . . . *gibberish* . . . [my name is] LaVern."

Then he pointed to her, asking "*Gibberish* [what is your name?]" All of a sudden she understood. His name was LaVern, and he wanted to know her name.

Very tentatively she said, "Suzanne."

"Suzanne," he said over and over in his deep, very American voice.

"No," she replied, and somehow was able to communicate that her family called her "Zanne."

"Zanne . . . Zanne . . ." he said over and over. It felt like he was caressing her with his voice.

"Oh no," she thought, "this has gone too far." In fear and trembling she turned and ran down the nearest street, not looking back, hoping and praying that he was not following her. How could she ever explain to her mother what had transpired and the emotions that had driven her to this point?

She had not returned to "their corner" since that day for fear of where her feelings might lead her, but oh, how she missed seeing him. Those brief encounters had become much more important to her than she had realized. Now it was Saturday and the cafe was filled with American servicemen, with their enthusiasm for life bubbling out all over the place. So many things they did and even said reminded Zanne of "her" American, increasing her desire to see him again, in spite of the opposition she knew she would encounter from her mother.

Her mind a thousand miles away, she started to clear dirty dishes off a table. Hearing the door of the cafe open she glanced up to see who had entered and suddenly the whole world stood still.

LAVERN !

LAVERN . . . LAVERN . . . standing there with that silly grin on his face that she had come to love.

O how abundant is your goodness that you have laid up for those who fear you, and accomplished for those who take refuge in you, in the sight of everyone!

Blessed be the LORD, for he has shown his steadfast love to me . . .

Psalm 31:19, 21

Chapter 12 –
Love Makes the World Go Round

Falling in love is a cascading waterfall of emotions that surprise, astonish, and grasp hold of a person's entire being. It is a rainbow of colors, as the water spills over the rocks of experience and wonder, gathering energy and strength, and in the process creating a deep pool, the force of which seems to lift one off the ground as if walking on air.

To love and to be loved in return is perhaps one of the greatest experiences in the life of a human being. It transcends all other emotions and feelings and gives one a glimpse of the divine. When in love, the world is viewed through rose-colored glasses and anything seems possible.

LaVern and Zanne were caught up in the miracle of loving and having that love returned. They were oblivious to what was around them, so wrapped up in each other were they.

It was a time of discovery; they both loved to dance, they both loved Glen Miller and "In the Mood" became "their song." Many nights they danced until they were completely exhausted, falling into each other's arms laughing themselves almost sick and reveling in the closeness they were experiencing so joyfully as their relationship deepened. They went for long walks, holding hands, communicating as best they could.

Zanne's parents were not happy about their romance. They did not trust the flamboyant American GI. They were sure that LaVern would take advantage of their innocent, convent educated daughter and then return to America leaving Zanne behind in Belgium, abandoned and heartbroken. Consequently, they insisted that Zanne's older sister serve as chaperone, accompanying them everywhere they went. It was her job to make sure they were never alone.

Over time, the lovers learned to communicate using both English and Flemish words, plus a lot of sign language and GI slang. Zanne's sister found it all very confusing, which greatly pleased the couple. Their times together, however, were not fulfilling. They yearned to be together without having to looking over their shoulder and always wondering what was being reported to Zanne's parents.

They secretly decided to run away together. Their intent at this time was not to marry, rather just to have some alone time.

LaVern gave Zanne money for their getaway, impressing upon her the need for secrecy. Zanne put it in her favorite hiding place amongst her handkerchiefs in one of her bureau drawers.

The next day, while her sister and mother were away from the cafe running errands, Zanne packed a small valise with just the bare essentials needed for a two to three-day stay. She then hid the bag in the back of her closet, where it would not be easily seen.

They did not set a definite date as everything depended upon when LaVern could commandeer a vehicle. In the midst of all the planning and intrigue, Zanne tried to appear calm, as if nothing out of the ordinary was going on. Beneath that cool exterior, however, Zanne was a wreck. Her heart told her one thing, and her sense of responsibility and upbringing told her another.

Zanne had never before gone against her parents' wishes. As a young child she had misbehaved as all children do and had been in trouble a few times at the convent school. However, what she was about to do now was a major step in becoming independent. She was afraid that it might be interpreted by her parents as outright rebellion. This she did not want. Rather, now that she was twenty years old, she needed them to respect her age and to accept that the time had come for her to make her own decisions regardless as to whether or not they were right or wrong.

She was deeply and hopelessly in love with LaVern and wanted her family to share in their joy in their love for each other. She was very aware of their reservations about him and their relationship and she knew their acceptance of his presence in their family life would not easily be forthcoming.

LaVern was different from anyone she had ever known. That was part of his charm. This man, molded by the prairie winds of Iowa, believed anything was possible. He was strong, determined and resolute. He knew the road ahead would be difficult, but he firmly believed that their love for each other was strong enough to overcome all obstacles and he was not about to back down.

With typical American optimism, he looked to the future, not the past. In his heart he was a builder, and dreamed of the life that he and Zanne would build together. They would find a new way of living that would not be molded by their surroundings, but by Zanne and LaVern themselves. Their dreams were many and filled with hope and promise.

Zanne loved to listen to him talk about their plans for a future together. He assured her that anything was possible in America if a person worked hard, lived frugally and saved their money. She believed that the American dream, promised in the many Hollywood films she had seen, was attainable.

She didn't think about the grief that would come to her and all her loved ones in Belgium if she left for the shores of America. Seeing the world through the rose-colored glasses of young passionate love, thoughts of grief and sorrow were non-existent. All she could think about was building a future with LaVern, and that future lay in America, the magical land of hope and promise.

In spite of their efforts to conceal their plans, Zanne's sister, who had come to know them as a couple quite well, suspected that something was going on. She also knew of Zanne's hiding place in amongst the handkerchiefs. One day when Zanne and her mother had gone shopping, her sister went to the bureau rummaging through the drawers. What she found astounded her. There in the soft folds of the hankies was money, lots and lots of money! There was only one source, one person that she knew of, who would have that kind amount of money . . . **LaVern!**

Her immediate reaction was to tell her mother. The more she thought about it, however, she realized it would be better to catch them in the act, so "she laid in wait," watching their every move, ready to pounce like a hungry lion stalking his prey.

She did not have to wait long. Two days later, she tip-toed into Zanne's room, as she had done previously, to check on the stash of money and found it to be gone.

"Ah, ah!" she thought. "I bet they are going to try to run away tonight."

She then went to her mother and told her all about her suspicions: finding the large amount of cash and then its disappearance. Her mother agreed with her assumptions and together they planned how to expose the young lovers.

They would supposedly retire for the night around ten o'clock, claiming extreme fatigue. This was not unusual because they were often exhausted with all the new business the American GI's had brought their way. As they had experienced one busy day after another, Zanne would expect them to fall into bed, immediately go to sleep, and thus plan accordingly. However, at about 10:45 pm the three of them (Zanne's mother, father and sister) would quietly return to the main floor, her parents hiding in the kitchen and her sister crouching in a corner of the dining room, from where she could see the whole area and someone coming down the stairs could not see her.

The three plotters were right on the mark about Zanne and LaVern's plans. The lovers had purposely not seen each other that day so as to not arouse any suspicions. Rather they had been together the day before, walking in one of the city parks, holding hands, talking, apparently like they usually did, hoping that it appeared to the sister that everything was normal. They were a little bit on the giddy side, but that was not unusual for them.

As they walked LaVern told Zanne his plans. He had gained access to a truck of one of his buddies, who said he could use it for two to three days. It was old, beat up, and a little loud, but it ran and that was what was important. LaVern would turn off the truck's motor a couple of blocks from the cafe and coast the rest of the way to the front door so he wouldn't be heard.

They planned to leave the following evening. Zanne told him she thought everyone would be asleep by 11:00 pm, at which time she would quietly sneak down the stairs and meet him at the door. Her valise was packed and she would put the money in it first thing the next morning. All she would have to do that night was to grab her case, her coat and go.

Zanne thought the next work day would never end. As usual they were very busy and normally that would make the time pass quickly, but it didn't that day. Also, she felt as if her parents were watching everything she did.

"Could they suspect something?" she wondered. "No, they couldn't possibly know anything."

"We have been so careful. It must be just nerves." She tried to assure herself, but to no avail. Finally, they closed up the cafe for the evening and retired to their respective rooms.

Zanne changed into a comfortable traveling outfit and then sat on the edge of her bed, waiting . . . waiting, watching the clock, certain that it had stopped: the hands moved so slowly. Finally, it was 10:55 pm . . . 10:56 pm . . . 10:57 pm . . . 10:58 pm . . . and then . . . 10:59 pm . . . . At last it was time, time to grab her things and go.

She got her valise from the back of the closet, checking to make sure the money was in it, and then put on her coat. She quietly walked across the room and out the door, and slowly began her descent down the stairs. Suddenly she stopped, horrified, scared and speechless. Standing there at the bottom of the stairs was not LaVern ready to carry her away, as they had planned, but rather her mother, father, and sister forming a wall between her and LaVern, who had just walked in the door.

"Just where do you think you are going, young lady, at this time of night with your valise?" asked her mother, in an agitated voice.

Zanne tried to answer, but she was so terrified that she could not even stammer a response. She looked to LaVern for help, and he immediately replied, "She is going with me," he said very firmly. "We need to be alone, completely alone in order to talk about our future. We cannot do that with her sister always listening to every word we say and watching everything we do!"

LaVern knew that Zanne's mother was not able to understand most of what he had said, but he could tell that she had comprehended enough to make her very angry.

By this time, Zanne had reached the bottom of the stairs and was running into LaVern's waiting arms. Before she could reach LaVern, however, her mother grabbed Zanne by her hair and dragged her screaming in pain into the adjoining dining room.

The two women wrestled together for what seemed like an eternity when all of a sudden Zanne broke free of her mother's hold on her hair and ran to LaVern. She picked up her valise and coat and they hurried out the door to the awaiting truck. At first the engine wouldn't start and Zanne thought, "Oh no, we are going to be stuck here. What are we going to do?"

Finally, however, after a few coaxing measures and words from LaVern, who was remaining incredibly calm during all of this, the engine fired and they were off, rattling down the street.

Above the noise of the engine, Zanne could hear her mother's voice as she screamed to Zanne's father, **"Call the police . . . call the police!"**

Questions That Arose From the Ashes of the Six Million

Where was God?

In the Holocaust, humanity turned it's back on God. We denied God and we spit on our neighbor. When we drove out the "Jew" we drove out Jesus, for Jesus was a Jew. We exiled ourselves from God, and the "presentness" of God in our living, and in that process lost our humanity: the image of God in us. God did not abandon us, humankind abandoned God.

The faith exhibited at Auschwitz and the faith and trust in Jesus Christ, God on the cross, sharing our human death, bears witness to the fact that the denial of God does not change the reality of God.

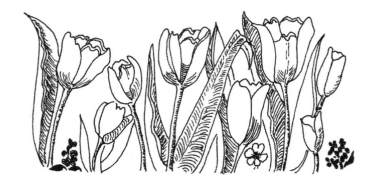

O LORD, my strong deliverer, you have covered my head in the day of battle.

Surely the righteous shall give thanks to your name; the upright shall live in your presence.

Psalm 140:7, 13

Chapter 13 – The Impossible Dream?

"You gotta have a dream. If you don't have a dream, how you gonna have a dream come true?" sings Bloody Mary in the much beloved Broadway musical, *South Pacific.*

To dream is to reach out in hope for the intangible; something not yet realized and sometimes seemingly impossible. Dreams reflect who we are, where we have been, where we hope to go and what we would like to accomplish. A life without dreams would be a barren wasteland of brokenness and deprivation.

Dreams often go by the wayside, laid to rest in the cemetery of "I can't do this, it is too hard for me, this will never happen."

There are those dreams, however, that come to fruition by the sheer will and grit of those who dare to pursue them, believing they are attainable.

As Zanne and LaVern sped across the Belgian countryside in the old truck that rattled, hissed and clanked, it was their dream of a future together that kept them focused on the task at hand, enabling them to cope with the crippling fear that threatened to defeat them. They were now committed to what lay ahead and *together*, they would face any roadblock thrown in their way. Their dreams were not going to be buried in the cemeteries of doubt and fear.

They were deeply shaken by what had transpired at Zanne's home. The anger and cruelty of her mother astonished Zanne. This made her face for the first time the reality of her parent's overwhelming opposition to her relationship with LaVern. The lovers had succeeded in making their planned escape, and they were alone, *finally* alone for the *first time* in the many months they had been seeing each other.

Everything that had happened seemed more like a movie rather than real life, it was surreal. On the one hand, they were joyful and excited to be "free." However, they were also filled with fear and dread. They knew that if her parents had indeed contacted the authorities, they would soon be in great jeopardy.

A strange quiet engulfed them, creating an uncomfortable silence between them which was new and unsettling. LaVern pushed the ancient engine of the old truck to its maximum capacity, believing that once they reached Holland and his base, they would be safe.

He was gravely mistaken, however. Shortly before they reached the border they began to hear the sirens of the Belgian police who were in hot pursuit, and driving vehicles that were in much better running condition than the worn out truck in which LaVern and Zanne were riding. Much to the couple's surprise, the Belgian authorities did not stop at the border, rather, they continued the chase into Holland and were soon joined by the military police from LaVern's base and their Hollander counterparts. Zanne's parents had called everyone they knew, accusing LaVern of kidnapping.

For three hours, the chase continued as they wound in and out through one sleepy village after another. The blasting sirens and flashing lights causing the locals to stop what they were doing, and stare unabashedly at the spectacle being played out in front of them. Finally the old truck gave out, the engine dying in the middle of an intersection, leaving LaVern and Zanne no option but to allow themselves to be taken into custody, reluctantly returning to Belgium. At the police station and later where LaVern was stationed, there ensued much haggling, shouted in various languages, with the young lovers insisting they had done nothing wrong and that Zanne had gone willingly with LaVern.

The protests of the lovers were ignored and LaVern was incarcerated, charged with kidnapping, a federal offense punishable by death. Since the incident occurred in a country just recently liberated from Nazi terrorism, the United States had to handle the situation very carefully, and thus the local authorities were encouraged to make the decisions regarding LaVern's future.

The US government did not want the populace to see them as overbearing conquerors, but rather as allies in the rebuilding of the heavily bombed and decimated country. Consequently two FBI agents, from New York City, who had been extensively trained in handling delicate diplomatic issues, were sent to help resolve the problem.

After many days of discussion, and much pleading by Zanne, tempers began to cool. Finally, Zanne's parents gave in and dropped the kidnapping charge. The American authorities also withdrew their accusations. The FBI agents talked at great length with LaVern. They wanted to be sure that he understood the seriousness of his actions and the possible ramifications that could have ensued as a result of his being so impetuous. They stressed the fact that the GI's represented The United States of America to the Europeans and how they conducted themselves would be the only picture that most people would ever have of the United States.

LaVern was awed by the responsibility laid upon his shoulders and resolved to be the best "ambassador" possible..

LaVern, Zanne, and her parents were exhausted physically, as sleep had eluded them due the chaos of the previous days. Emotionally spent, they returned to Zanne's home, wondering what to do next. It was not a comfortable time for any of them.

LaVern knew that somehow he had to come to terms with Zanne's parents and help them to see how much he loved and cared for their daughter. Now that his intentions were out in the open he wanted to build a good relationship with them. It started with his name.

Zanne's family thought LaVern was a ridiculous name for a man and they insisted on calling him "Jimmy," which for some unknown reason sounded better to them. From then on they were referred to as "Jimmy" and Zanne and were finally allowed to be alone without the presence of Zanne's sister.

LaVern was so grateful for their apparent acceptance of him that one morning he appeared at their home with a beautiful full-length fur coat for Zanne's mother. She was thrilled beyond words. Not wanting to slight Zanne's sister, who had been their constant companion for so long, he also gifted her with a fur coat a few days later.

The turning point in LaVern's relationship with Zanne's parents came, however when he produced the biggest surprise of all. For months, Zanne's father had been talking about getting a pet. LaVern was aware of this and so he went to great lengths to find an adorable little puppy, which he, in grateful humbleness, presented to her father.

That did it! Her father said in a loud voice, "Oh let them get married!"

LaVern acted immediately, and getting down on one knee he formally proposed.

Upon the bestowal of approval and blessing of their union by Zanne's parents their impossible dream became a reality.

Zanne and "Jimmy" were married on May 21, 1946, in a simple civil ceremony.

"You gotta have a dream. If you don't have a dream, how you gonna have a dream come true?"

Married May 21, 1946

Questions That Arose From the Ashes of the Six Million

Responsibility

Responsibility is a very complicated issue. You cannot blame a Hitler when millions of people were taken by trains, "assisted" by local guards and train engineers.

A Holocaust Survivor

The question is not, "Why is there undeserved suffering?" but "why is there man?" He who asks the question about injustice in history really asks; "Why a world? Why creation?"

God's very mercy and forbearance, his very love for humankind necessitates the abandonment of some to a fate that they may well experience as divine indifference to justice and human suffering.

He who demands justice of God must give up humankind; he who asks for God's love and mercy beyond justice, must accept suffering.

Eleizer Berkovits, Jewish Theologian

I trusted in your steadfast love; my heart shall rejoice in your salvation.

I will sing to the LORD, because he has dealt bountifully with me.

Psalm 13:5, 6

Chapter 14 – Separation

A law of physics states that to every action there is a reaction. If the rope of a church bell is pulled, the bell will ring. If someone steps on the gas pedal of a car, the car will move forward or backward, depending on which gear is engaged. If a freshly painted surface is touched, a mark will be left. Often that reaction causes a change to occur that cannot be reversed and must be dealt with accordingly.

The same principle applies to human living. The decisions we make, either good or bad, all come with consequences, consequences that often set into motion a sequence of events which are beyond our control.

A short time after they were married the army informed LaVern that Zanne was scheduled for transport to the United States, by ship, along with 250 other war brides and their children. They were dismayed by this news. They knew this was coming, but they never dreamed that it would materialize so quickly. LaVern had six months left in his tour of duty in Europe. Consequently, this summons meant that Zanne would have to travel alone, to this strange new country, meeting LaVern's family for the first time, without LaVern's support, and thus having to struggle by herself to adjust to a whole new world.

It was all very daunting. Everything she knew about America came from the films she had seen. She possessed no real knowledge or understanding of American customs and culture. She did not doubt her love for LaVern, nor her belief that they were meant to be together. For the first time in their relationship, however, she was apprehensive about the future.

To complicate things further, she had just discovered that she was pregnant! She and LaVern were thrilled, but they were concerned about how she would withstand the Atlantic crossing. Much to their relief, Zanne was informed that she and each of the women on the ship would be accompanied by a personal attendant that would help with language difficulties and see to their being united with their corresponding American families. This greatly relieved LaVern as he was deeply concerned about Zanne's ability to adjust and find her way without him.

Zanne was also worried about her ability to communicate. Her knowledge of English was mostly GI talk, a language unto its own, with some words that were not repeatable in "polite society."

One day as they were discussing this problem, LaVern said,

"You like baloney and it is the same word in English. If something is said to you that you don't understand, just say, 'Oh, Baloney!'"

This advice served her well in the months to come. As she adjusted to life in America, she often found herself saying, "Oh, Baloney!"

Each time she did her mother-in-would laugh heartily, a warm, accepting laugh that would brighten the day and make Zanne feel loved and understood.

The days passed quickly, as Zanne prepared for her new adventure. She could hardly believe it. She was actually going to be living in America. She continued to be concerned about all the things she didn't know and the language difficulty, but her excitement about living in "movie land" outweighed her concerns.

It was hard to believe this was happening to her. The farthest from home she had ever been was to the convent school, which was only a few miles from her town, but now she would be traveling thousands of miles, crossing the broad expanse of the Atlantic Ocean in the process.

She tried not to think about leaving her family. She knew her parents were sad about her going so far away, wondering if they would ever see their daughter again. Not much was said as she went about the business of packing and making decisions on what to take and what to leave behind, but her impending departure hung in the air, like an unwelcomed guest.

Sensing her parent's grief, she kept her excitement to herself, but she couldn't help but hum happy tunes as she packed her bags and made the other necessary arrangements. She was instructed by the army to provide her own transportation to Paris. Paris! How exciting was that? From there she would be bussed, along with the other women, to the port from which they would embark.

The day of her departure for Paris arrived much too quickly. As she watched her father load her suitcases into the car she reflected on the first time she saw LaVern, his tentative smile and wave, wasn't that just yesterday?

Saying goodbye to LaVern was agony beyond words. The six months ahead of her without LaVern seemed like an eternity. How would she survive? He had become her whole world and now she was being ripped away from him and everything she had ever known and cared about.

Quiet prevailed as they sped on their way to Paris, each wrapped up in their own thoughts. Her parent's grief at having to say goodbye, readily apparent. However, it was not just seeing Zanne off that saddened them. One of her sisters was also leaving that same day for South Africa! Would they ever see their two daughters again? That question hung like a pall over them, making it impossible to enjoy the sights of that great city.

After a tearful farewell, Zanne's parents left the hotel where Zanne would spend the night, her mother crying, uncontrollably. Saying goodbye to two daughters headed for parts unknown on the same day was almost more than she could bear. Their return trip to Belgium was a silent one, as both of her parents contemplated the future for them and their daughters.

Zanne was alone, really all alone for the first time in her entire life and she was afraid, deeply afraid.

What would the days ahead bring?

What kind of sailor would she be?

Would she like her personal attendant and feel comfortable with her?

Would she like her fellow shipmates?

What was it like to be on a big ship?

Was she going to be seasick?

And what is America like?

Will it be like what she saw in the movies?

Will she like LaVern's family?

Will they like her?

What will she do if she can't stand them?

The questions went on and on, driving her crazy.

"I should have asked all those questions before I committed myself to this insane adventure," she reasoned.

"What am I doing here all by myself in this beautiful and yet strange city," she asked herself as she began to question her actions and decisions.

Having worked herself into a frenzy, she went over to the window to open it, hoping that a breath of fresh air would help to clear her head. As she looked out onto the street, she could not believe what she saw.

"I'm dreaming," she thought. "All of my worrying has gotten the better of me and my vivid imagination has taken hold."

She looked again, and nothing had changed. Standing beneath her window, with that lopsided grin so endearing to her was *LaVern!*

She ran out of her room, bounding down the spiral staircase, running headlong into his waiting arms, sobbing hysterically and clinging to him as if he were the only thing in the world that was solid and sure.

In between the sobs she cried out, "What are you doing here? How did you get here? How did you know where I was? Oh, LaVern, I love you so much."

"Please tell me everything is going to be alright, that I am going to love America and your family. I am so afraid, so afraid. Do I have to go alone? Can't you come with me?"

After several moments in his comforting arms, she managed to calm down. As he tenderly wiped the tears from her eyes he explained his presence. Sensing Zanne's unspoken fears he had gone to his CO, begging him to grant him a twenty-four-hour pass. He drove to Paris like a madman, hoping he would reach Zanne before she left the city. From the army relocation authorities, he was able to ascertain at which hotel she would be staying, and *viola,* here he was in person, holding her in his embrace, bringing calm to her storm.

He reminded her of their dream of a life together. That they believed it was meant to be; it was their destiny. He assured Zanne that his parents would welcome her with open arms and loving hearts. He acknowledged her fears and said they were justified, but he knew she was strong and would prevail.

They talked and talked throughout the night, locked in each other's arms, wishing that dawn would never come. However as the sun appeared on the eastern horizon, they arose, resolute, strong and sure, their love for each other having reached a new plateau. Zanne was emboldened by LaVern's confidence in her and her ability to cope with what lay ahead. He knew his family would take loving care of her and he was able to assure Zanne of their acceptance of her as his wife and their new daughter.

As she boarded the bus later that morning, with the other wives, she looked back at her beloved husband with those luminous eyes that had captured him in the beginning. Taking a big breath, she managed a smile and waving goodbye she disappeared into the confines of the vehicle, her tears hidden by the tinted glass of the bus windows.

Questions That Arose From the Ashes of the Six Million

Where is God?

That man may be, God must absent himself; that man may not perish in the tragic absurdity of his own making, God must remain present. The God of history must be absent and present concurrently."

Elizer Berkovits, Jewish Theologian

If man is to remain the creature as created by God, then God must absent God's self – in other words, God must allow man to be man and not interfere with humanity's free will.

That God must be absent and present concurrently is a concept almost impossible to grasp. A person of faith struggles with this, and while not able to fully comprehend it, acknowledges the necessity for absence and presence. That recognition does not ease suffering or pain or answer all the questions. However, perhaps it enables one to begin to accept that God is the creator and man is God's creation and that there is a difference.

It is not for the created to know the mind of God, but to experience God's love and acceptance of us as his own "little ones," recipients of God's abundant grace.

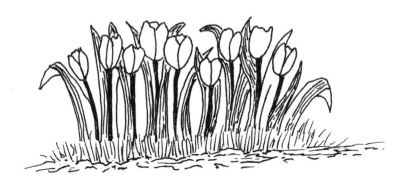

(The LORD) did not hide his face from me, but heard when I cried to him.

All the ends of the earth shall remember and turn to the LORD; and all the families of the nations shall worship before him. For dominion belongs to the LORD, and he rules over the nations.

Psalm 22:24b, 27-28

Chapter 15 – As Time Goes By

For everything there is season, and a time
   for every matter under heaven:
a time to be born, and a time to die;
a time to plant, and a time to pluck up
   what is planted;
a time to kill, and a time to heal;
a time to break down, and a time to build up;
a time to weep, and a time to laugh;
a time to mourn, and a time to dance . . .
a time to seek, and a time to lose . . .
a time to love, and a time to hate;
a time for war, and a time for peace.

Ecclesiastes 3

LaVern drove slowly back to his base in Holland. He was already missing Zanne's luminous eyes and infectious laughter, her engaging smile and her optimistic outlook on life. His mind was a whirling mass of thoughts, images, and truths concerning their relationship and their future together. The words of the book of Ecclesiastes in the Bible suddenly came to him, reminding him that everything has its time. Having grown up on a farm he had a better understanding of those words than most people.

> **"For everything there is a season, and a time
> for every matter under heaven."**

He had experienced the marvelous season of falling headlong in love and all the glorious emotions that come with it. His heart was so full he felt as if it might burst. Zanne had become his whole world. How was he ever going to survive the months that lay ahead of him without her presence in his life?

It was a time to weep, for he felt so alone, but it was also a time to laugh as he remembered some of the crazy things they had done together. He smiled as he thought about the wonderful evenings when they danced the night away to Glenn Miller's "In the Mood," their struggle to understand each other's language and their adventurous failed attempt at running away together.

There were moments, however when other memories drowned out the laughter of their romance. He remembered, with shame, his first time in combat when he experienced a fear so great that it took possession of his entire being and he lost control of his bodily functions. He had learned, however, that fear was an ally, for it sharpened his senses, strengthened his resolve and instilled in him a surprising courage that he didn't know he possessed.

He had survived the killing fields of Europe and had come face to face with the devil in the chamber of horrors known as Buchenwald. He followed orders as any good soldier does. It had been a time to kill, but the guilt and shame of following those orders would haunt him for the rest of his life.

The killing now over, it was a time to heal, to build up what had been broken down, body and spirit alike. Upon his return to his base, he resumed his trips to the DP camp. Each time he passed "their corner," though he knew she would not be there, he still looked for Zanne, and he was filled with unbearable longing. She was his heart and soul and he knew he would not be whole again until they were finally together.

The months spent without Zanne became his "time to seek." In the heat of passion that overcomes young lovers, common sense goes out the window. They are consumed by what is happening in their rose colored world. All they want to do is explore, explore each other's mind, soul and body.

During the five months he was required to remain on active duty in Holland and Belgium he worked to seek a better understanding of what had transpired between them. With a clear head and his emotions somewhat under control, he came to some startling conclusions. He had just assumed that they would make their home in The United States. The more he thought about it, the more he realized his selfishness. He had never asked her what she wanted to do. He had given no thought or consideration to the grief and sadness she would experience by leaving her family and all she had ever known.

He looked back on his first impressions of Europe and how totally different it was from the prairies and cornfields of Iowa. He felt penned in by the density of the population, and he yearned deeply for the wide open spaces of the Midwest. He felt like he didn't belong, and never would completely understand how Europeans thought and acted as they did because he didn't share their history. He would always be the outsider.

Would it not be the same for Zanne? He had never considered it. He remembered the look of panic and fear in her beautiful face as she board the bus with the other war brides bound for the ship that would take her thousands of miles across wind and sea, to a land completely foreign to her, to people that were strangers and a culture, never before experienced.

"What have I done," he asked himself, "Oh what have I done?"

Sing praises to the LORD, O you faithful ones, and give thanks to his holy name. Weeping may linger for the night, but joy comes with the morning.

Psalm 30:4, 5b

Chapter 16 – The New World

The human mind is an awesome creation. If its potential could be fully recognized and used, the word "impossible" would not be in our vocabulary. Feats of incredible daring, strength and courage give rise to the fact that what appears to be impossible is achievable if the mind can overcome the road-blocks placed in its path; thus the axiom, "mind over matter."

There are untold numbers of stories about heroic feats, in which the mind made the body do what seemed to be impossible, rescue missions being a prime example of this.

There are other times when the mind goes into a preserva-tion mode in order to save one's sanity. Sometimes when peo-ple experience a serious accident involving terrible injuries and tragic loss, amnesia will occur, giving the brain a chance to rest and recoup.

Suzie remembers very little about her ocean crossing. It is all a blur. She remembers being periodically sick, however, she never knew if it was because of rough seas, morning sickness or fear of what she would meet in the new world that she would soon encounter. She thinks it took two weeks to make the voy-age, but she isn't sure of that fact.

What she vividly remembers, was her eagerness to get off the boat! Much to her dismay upon their arrival in New York City, their ship was quarantined because many of the children on board had an illness that could not be explained, and some of them had died from the disease. Their boat was anchored at the base of the Statue of Liberty for two weeks! Zanne just about went nuts. She was so tired of the cramped quarters, the food, and the smells. To top it off, her morning sickness had worsened. She was thoroughly miserable and filled with self-pity which was not like her at all as she was usually a very optimistic person.

Finally the quarantine was lifted and they were allowed to disembark, never knowing what the sickness was that had held them captive for two weeks. As she walked down the gangplank, she heard the latest hit song of the Andrew Sisters being sung for them as a welcome to America gesture. It was one of her favorites and it was being sung by the Andrew Sisters themselves! She had long been a fan of theirs and to see them in person was really exciting.

With her head still in the stars, she and her personal attendant, who had made all the travel arrangements for the two of them, boarded a train bound for Chicago. That trip is also a blur for her. There was just too much for her to assimilate. Her brain was on overload. The differences between what she had imagined America to be like, what Hollywood promised, and what she was now seeing and experiencing, was just too much for her to fully comprehend and digest. Her morning sickness continued, making travel very difficult.

Chicago was as far as her personal attendant could go with her. She put Zanne on a train headed for Mason City, Iowa, assuring her that she had been in contact with LaVern's family and that they were planning to be at the station in Mason City to meet her.

Again, she was all alone in a strange land, and everything was so different, *so different!*

Clickety-clack, clickety-clack, the sound of the train speeding along its track, brought to Zanne's mind memories and emotions that had been set aside in all the excitement surrounding their plans for the future. As she sat silently, looking out the train window, her thoughts turned to other trains, trains of cattle cars filled with people whose only crime was their lineage.

She remembered the terrible fear that her family had lived with, the fear that their mother, who was part Jewish, might be taken from them and shoved into one of those cars that would carry her to her death. As the miles sped by she began to relive some of her war experiences, bringing her to tears. Would she ever be able to get past the hatred and terror that she carried deep within her?

She was so engrossed in her thoughts that she did not realize that the train had begun to slow down until the conductor came through the car in which she was riding, and with a loud voice was announcing;

"Mason City, next stop, Mason City! Mason City! Next stop!"

She gathered up all her things, took a big breath and walked down the car steps to the platform. There in front of her stood four people who somewhat looked like LaVern, a motherly appearing person, a father and two children. The mother, with a warm and welcoming smile and outstretched arms exclaimed, "You must be Suzie! Welcome to Iowa, Suzie!" And with that greeting came a big hug.

Zanne wanted to say, "My name is Zanne," but she didn't know the words to use and so she just smiled in acknowledgment. In some ways, it seemed appropriate, a new world, and a new name. Zanne belonged to the old world and the name Suzie sounded very American. She has been Suzie ever since, Zanne being a name from her past, a name that belonged to another time and place.

They retrieved her other bags from baggage claim and headed for the parking lot, with Suzie trailing behind. She was trying to keep up their fast pace but wanted to also take in the sights and sounds of this American city she would be living near.

It was very different from Rieme-Ertvelde. Most of the buildings were only one or two stories high, with flat roofs. She thought they were kind of ugly!

The train station was located in a part of the town that had seen better days. In Belgium and throughout Europe the railroad depots were always located in the heart of the city, surrounded by beautiful buildings and parks.

She was astonished at how many cars there were, they were everywhere. Very few people in her town owned cars. They depended on public transit to go places, but it seemed as though everyone in Mason City had their own car!

They reached the White's car, a big four-door sedan. After putting all her things in its roomy trunk, they piled into the vehicle and headed north, bound for the town of Grafton and from there on to the farm where LaVern had spent his childhood.

As Suzie recalls her trip from downtown Mason City to the farmlands around Grafton, she becomes very quiet.

"It wasn't anything like what I had imagined," she says pensively. "It was miles and miles of open spaces. I had always lived in a highly populated area, with lots of people on the streets and the buildings standing close to each other. I found the openness of the prairie to be frightening and very disturbing. There were no boundaries, just fences. It was all very unnerving and oh, how I missed LaVern. He hadn't told me about the wide open spaces. He took the prairie for granted, and it was so familiar to him that he didn't think about how different it would seem to me."

"The county side was unlike anything I had ever known," she continues. She and LaVern had never really talked about the differences in their two countries and their respective cultures. They had just assumed that everything would work out because they were in love! In the rose-colored world of grand passion in which they had been living, there were no storm clouds, just laughter, smiles, joy, and happiness. Now a little drop of doubt entered her mind causing anxiousness.

[I have been told that Suzie's reaction to the wide open spaces found in this country is quite common among people coming from Europe for the first time. They find the vastness of the countryside to be frightening, having always lived in densely populated areas, where the only open space to be found was in the city parks which had boundaries, were immaculately groomed and always full of people.]

Everywhere she looked she saw fields of corn growing in the Iowa sun, the prairie winds rustling through the stalks, with the tassels adorning the tops of the giant plants, busily fertilizing the kernels of corn being born in the cobs below. The stalks were tall and stately, vivid green in color, stretching in long rows as far as the eye could see.

It was an amazing sight. She had never seen corn in the field before and had never thought if it being grown for human consumption. Rather, in Europe, the grain is strictly raised for animal feed. Over time, she has learned to like corn, especially on the cob and was dumbfounded and thrilled with popcorn. She never tires of watching it being made. To see the kernels of corn puffing up to three times their size, as they pop, remains a miracle in Suzie's eyes.

Upon arrival at the farm, Suzie immediately needed to use the bathroom. She asked in broken English where the toilet was and Mrs. White pointed to a little wooden shed in back of the house. Suzie thought she must have misunderstood, but Mrs. White insisted that was it. Suzie's home in Belgium had indoor plumbing. She had never seen an outhouse in her whole life. She opened the door and peered inside. Oh, the smell, but she could tell this was the place and she was desperate. Upon finishing she ran into the house to the room appointed for her, throwing herself on the bed, sobbing. She had never felt so alone in her entire life.

"What have I done?" She sobbed, "Oh, what have I done?"

Questions That Arose From the Ashes of the Six Million

Who is Responsible for the Holocaust?

While people cry out for freedom, when faced with the gift of this complete freedom, humanity has difficulty with the obligations that are a part of the gift. When one is able to make history, then one is also responsible for the outcome of the history making. The Holocaust is the consequence of humanity's complete freedom and subsequent lack of tending to the responsibilities that come with it.

God is responsible for the Holocaust because God made the human race responsible at the time of creation.

"Fill the earth and subdue it; and have dominion over the fish of the sea and over the birds of the air and over every living thing that moves upon the earth."

Genesis 1:28

The consequence of such a creation is that God cannot and must not intervene at every whim of humanity. Does this mean then that God has set the world in motion and walked away from it? Absolutely not! Jesus Christ is the answer to that question; the Word made flesh that dwelled among us. Christ is the living witness that God continues to be involved in all aspects of human life, especially in death and suffering.

The Holocaust raises questions about this involvement that can never be answered to anyone's satisfaction, but it is those very questions that lead us to seek the truth and to come face to face with the responsibilities that accompany God's gift of free will.

God is responsible for the Holocaust because the power to make history was given to all humanity at creation.

The cry that rises out of those terrible years in Germany is, "Never Again!" But the possibility of it happening again is there, as long as humanity refuses to recognize and accept the responsibilities that accompany God's gift of free will.

Epilog

LaVern returned home to the prairies of Iowa in time to witness the birth of his first born child, a boy, whom they named Jerry, and who was definitely a Chalmet (Suzie's family name). One year and one day later a baby girl, named Janice, looking just like the Whites, came into the world, thus making life very busy, especially for Suzie.

LaVern's family assumed that when he came back from the war he would return to farming, which he initially did, and at the same time he also managed the lumber yard in Grafton. However his war experiences and exposure to the world beyond Grafton had changed him. His horizons had been broadened, and he discovered he had many interests aside from farming that he wished to pursue.

Thinking about the future and what it held for Suzie and him and their children, he found himself reflecting on his experiences on the killing fields of Europe. As the battles raged around him, his thoughts had turned to his prairie upbringing. The peace that accompanied those farm memories had helped to preserve his sanity in the midst of the madness of modem warfare. He began to realize how fortunate he was to have been raised on a farm, and increasingly grateful for the values installed in him and the lessons about life and living he had assimilated during those early formative years.

His war experiences had been terrifying, and he had been witness to things so horrible he couldn't even speak of them, and yet it proved to be a time of great personal growth He discovered that there was more to LaVern White than he had ever imagined and would not have known if he had not been a part of that great conflict. It had, indeed, made a man out of him, giving him the courage to declare to his family that farming was not what he wanted do for the rest of his life.

His time spent in reflection, however, made him realize that the farm was too much a part of him to turn his back on that life and completely walk away from it; thus he became rural mail carrier for the United States Postal Service, remaining in that position until his retirement in 1990. It was an ideal vocation for him, as it enabled him to be meaningfully involved in the agricultural life of his community, while still pursuing his other interests.

In the years that followed, much of his time was devoted to remodeling and building homes in the Grafton area. He also became very skilled at refinishing furniture as well. He eventually opened his own auction business, and enjoyed twenty very successful years of auctioneering throughout the entire country. He became especially fond of, and gained extensive knowledge in carnival glass, earning a reputation for being an expert in that field. At one point in time, he and Suzie together owned and operated an antique shop, appropriately named, "Past Time Antiques."

He took great pride in his service to his country, as reflected in his being a member of, and participating in, the activities of the *American Legion,* in Grafton. He was also a lifetime member of the *Veterans of Foreign Wars,* in Mason City, Iowa.

Suzie devoted her life to the raising of their children and being the supportive wife of her very busy and energetic husband. She and LaVern shared a love of antiques, and due to her European background, she had a vast knowledge of the value of the various items they bought and sold.

Their business required a lot of traveling, and this pleased them as they both love to go new places and meet new people. As they drove along the highways and byways of this vast nation, they would often reminisce about their wild ride through the Belgian countryside with the authorities in hot pursuit. Their hysterical laughter that always followed the sharing of that memory was one of their moments in time, the significance of which only they could appreciate.

Suzie also discovered that she had a flare for decorating, and designed the interiors for most of the houses that LaVern built, many of which they lived in for a while before selling them and moving on. She loves bluebirds and has an untold number of paintings of those spectacular birds, beautifully framed by LaVern. The paintings were lovingly hung on the walls throughout their homes. Her decorating style, understandably, reflected her heritage. Upon entering their home a person could easily experience a sense of having crossed the Atlantic, transported into another world and culture.

Those same beautiful pictures of Suzie's precious bluebirds now adorn the walls of her room in the nursing home in which she currently resides. Along with the bluebirds are many pictures of her family.

LaVern and Suzie loved to dance and continued to do so until it was no longer possible for LaVern to navigate the dance floor. Glen Miller's "In the Mood" remained their favorite. People often remark on what a striking couple they made, especially noting Suzie's incredible beauty.

It is that beauty and those captivating eyes that kept LaVern enchanted through all their married years. He continued to worship the ground she walked on, and experienced the sensation of being thunderstruck by the sight of those incredible, luminous eyes gazing at him. The vision of her standing on that Belgian street comer, so long ago, and waving at him, as he drove by, was burned into his memory as if it only happened yesterday.

Suzie has spent the last seventy years learning to adapt to life in America. However, she still struggles with the image projected by the movie industry that had shaped her ideas of the kind of life she would experience in this country, and the reality of American life she encountered, especially on the farm.

LaVern had never completely recovered from his remorse at having ripped Suzie away from her family, her country, and all she had ever known. That remorse was a part of the fabric of their marriage.

As LaVern feared, there were times when Suzie felt like an outsider. She is very much aware that she is different from her Grafton counterparts. Her European upbringing, steeped in centuries old traditions and the terrifying war experiences of her youth can never truly be understood by her American friends and family.

Fortunately, during the ensuing years following Suzie's departure for the US one of her brothers visited LaVern and Suzie several times, and they in turn, were able to return to Belgium on three different occasions. Suzie is very grateful for those opportunities to visit her family and old friends. She discovered, however, that she had lived long enough in America, that in returning to her parental home, she found herself to be as much the outsider as she experiences in Grafton. Caught between the two worlds, with one foot in Europe and the other firmly planted on American soil; she feels as if she is being torn apart.

When she experiences one of those moments of disorientation, she often lashes out in anger and frustration, or becomes very quiet and withdraws into herself.

She remains a woman of mystery to many, but to her husband she was like a precious china doll, to be cherished and loved. Together they shared a past known only to them, a life uniquely lived, forever marked by the war that brought them together.

Conclusion

The Holocaust was a totally unique occurrence in the history of humankind. Episodes of genocide have transpired in various wars and conflicts, but never before or since World War II has there been an orchestrated plan, such as the German Nazi government had in place, to annihilate an entire race of people.

The "The Final Solution," as it was called, to the "Jewish problem" involved the entire population, from the highest authority down to the German "hausfrau," who hid in silence, behind locked doors, as neighbors were dragged from their homes and shoved into waiting trucks. It was common knowledge that the destination of those vehicles was the train station where the captives were loaded into cattle cars, forming long trains, which would haul them to the death camps in the east.

With German precision and thoroughness, every step in the process was carefully planned, down to the last detail. This included making the best possible use of the "leftovers," such as glasses, gold dental crowns (pulled from the mouths of the corpses before they were transported to the crematories), hair, shoes, etc. Nothing was "wasted."

The magnitude of such planning and the incredible intent of one nation to exterminate an entire race, is beyond human comprehension, thus it has been called "THE" Holocaust, in other words, the holocaust of all holocausts.

Through the centuries, the Exodus (Moses leading the people of Israel out of bondage, in Egypt, to the Promised Land) has been celebrated as the great saving event in Jewish history. Intricately woven into the fabric of their worship liturgy are remembrances of the great happening.

Since 1945, however, the liturgy has been reworked in order to incorporate the Holocaust experiences and reflections of the remnant that survived the camps. While there were those who cried out to God in anger and frustration, there were many survivors who did not think that God had abandoned them, rather that God was at work creating God's good from the ashes. It is their belief that Hitler's obsession with eradicating the "Jewish menace" brought about his defeat, thus saving the world from Nazi domination.

The generation that participated in that great conflict is quickly fading from our midst and the memories of their experiences are fading with them. It is our sacred calling to document and record their stories, that their sacrifice not go unheeded, but rather be a reminder that we must be watchful guardians of the cherished truths for which they fought and died. We are bound by their commitment to God and country to see to it that the atrocities they witnessed not be repeated.

From the ashes of the death camps comes the agonizing cry, "NEVER AGAIN, NEVER AGAIN!"

Amidst the discoveries of the death camps and the horrors found therein, a little stalk of blooming spring love pushed its way up through the ashes, dispelling the darkness of the smoke created by the crematories, a shining beacon of light in the pervasive doom and gloom. LaVern and Suzie's story of love and dreams of a future together was one of many romances which blossomed during those tormented times in which they found themselves.

The senses of young lovers during those turbulent days were on overload, their emotions running at warp speed because of the unusual circumstances that surrounded them. Death was everywhere! Therefore, the bright and beautiful flower of their growing love for each other brought a glimmer of hope to the darkness which they had experienced in the terrible closing days of the war. Their love was a ray of sunshine, a promise of the return to a "normal" life, guiding them along the path to the fulfillment of their dreams.

Unlike many of the romances that occurred during that time, however, LaVern and Suzie's desire to be together and their attempt to achieve that goal turned into an incident involving the governments of the United States and the Allies. The intrigue that encircled them and the possible international ramifications of their actions make their story uniquely compelling. Their chance meeting on a street corner, LaVern falling madly in love with Suzie at first sight, her parents disapproval of their relationship, and the lovers desperate attempt to run away together, reads like a movie script.

When Suzie speaks of those early days of the discovery of their love for each other there is a twinkle in those beautiful eyes that captivated LaVern's heart so many years ago, and a knowing smile on her lips. One cannot help but wonder what secrets lay behind that smile.

Never Again will there be a romance quite like theirs, with all the intrigue and excitement of a spy thriller, combined with the explosive passion found only in the very young. It is the story of two ordinary people, who have experienced a most extraordinary life.